Still Called by Name

Other books by
Fr. Dominic Grassi

Bumping into God

Bumping into God Again

Do You Love Me?

S✝ILL CALLED

WHY I LOVE
BEING A PRIEST
DOMINIC GRASSI

BY NAME

LoyolaPress.

CHICAGO

LOYOLAPRESS.
3441 N. ASHLAND AVENUE
CHICAGO, ILLINOIS 60657
(800) 621-1008
WWW.LOYOLABOOKS.ORG

Jacket and interior design by Megan Duffy Rostan
Jacket photography: Phil Martin

Library of Congress Cataloging-in-Publication Data
Grassi, Dominic.
   Still called by name : why I love being a priest / Dominic Grassi.
     p.   cm.
   ISBN 0-8294-1715-X
   1. Pastoral theology—Catholic Church.   2. Grassi, Dominic.
3. Catholic Church—Clergy—Biography.   I. Title.
   BX1913.G686 2003
   282'.092—dc21   2003011284

Printed in the United States of America
03 04 05 06 07 08 09 10 M-V 10 9 8 7 6 5 4 3 2 1

❃❃❃❃❃❃❃

Italians believe that the mother of a priest will
automatically enter heaven. This book is dedicated
to my mother. My help has not been necessary.

❃❃❃❃❃❃❃

CONTENTS

Part Three: The Grace That Appears

Acknowledgments

I want to thank Joe Durepos and all of the staff of Loyola Press. They were the genesis of this book. With all the headlines and media coverage of scandal in the priesthood and in the church, their concern for me led to conversations, which in turn led to the conviction that people want to know their priests better. This book is an attempt to help them accomplish that.

Vinita Wright takes my words and transforms them into what I wanted to say in a way they can be understood. Now that's an editor.

My family continues, now through another generation, to support me. As the late Fr. John Klein used to say, a healthy priest has healthy family relationships to fall back on. He also would say, "I wouldn't want to miss the next five years for anything." I will be the one who misses sharing them with him.

For fifteen years my priesthood has been gloriously intertwined with the lives of the faith-filled parishioners of St. Josaphat Parish in Chicago. Together we have made it "a church to come home to." Every day they ordain me. Together we have created a parish that is warm and welcoming. They continue to give me so much of themselves and to teach me much about our faith.

On Being Called by Name

It all came into focus for me one night in a neighborhood Italian restaurant, a fitting place for it to happen. There, the owners know me by name. An etching of St. Josaphat Church, where I have been pastor for more than fifteen years, hangs on the wall at the side of the bar. This restaurant is as good a symbol as any of the urban priesthood I have aspired to and dreamed about all my life.

On this particular evening I found myself sitting like a silent referee between two close friends whose paths were diverging right before my eyes.

Over the years we had shared much of our priesthood. As teachers and administrators of the high school seminary where we worked, we combined our creative talents in liturgies and retreats and classes. Our styles complemented one another. Our disagreements were more often about style than substance. Even when our ministries took us to other assignments, we looked forward to our dinners together, when we would "solve all the problems of the church" before dessert arrived.

Over time our friendship had sustained us. One of us had moved from being a radical high school seminary professor to becoming a bishop, making all the perfunctory and necessary stops along the way. The other had just returned from a six-month sabbatical after abruptly ending his pastorate in an exceptionally vibrant African American parish. While he was away he had made the choice to leave the priesthood. Simply stated, he had fallen out of love with the priesthood. Issues such as the ban on married clergy and on women priests and the ongoing racial injustice in the church made it harder— and finally impossible—for him to be a public minister anymore. It was a decision that had been a long time in the making.

This was our first dinner together since our friend had returned from his sabbatical. All I could do was watch in silence as two worldviews collided. One view was that the church had abandoned the poor, had denied women their rightful place, and continued to oppress minorities by condoning injustice. The other view was that the church was the bastion of truth, the stronghold of faith, and the institution that would protect us from our own self-inflicted chaos. One friend saw members of the hierarchy as self-serving careerists, out of touch and cowardly, who prevented him from ministering effectively. The other saw himself as part of a select group of dedicated, hard-working men committed to the leadership of the church.

Before long, napkins were being tossed onto plates for emphasis. Voices rose. Body language clearly communicated a widening chasm between them. Finally, each shook his head in disbelief at the other's intractable position. It was then that they both turned and looked at me, remembering suddenly that I was sitting between them.

At that moment I realized how miserably alone I felt. Clearly my priesthood had led me to a different place than theirs had led them. I was not ready to abandon the priesthood, nor did I want to accept what it had become for too many people. What I did know for sure was that mine was no longer the priesthood into which I had been ordained in the heady, hopeful, and naive decade of the seventies. But then again, I also realized that I am no longer the person I was then.

I knew in my heart that this would be the last time, after countless movies and dinners and discussions, that the three of us would ever talk about the priesthood from anywhere close to the same perspective. Years ago, our perspectives had grown out of our shared experiences. This was no longer true, and I was filled with sadness. At that moment I began to mourn a palpable loss in my life.

For some inexplicable reason, God has called me to be a priest. In fact, I have been that priest for more than half of my life. I will always be a priest. What that means, and will mean, I cannot say for sure. But given what God has done for me and asked of me over the years, I know that the priestly life will never be dull.

What is more important—and just as inexplicable—is that I know I will never be abandoned by the God whose unconditional love is at the very core of the gospel I preach. This one belief holds me securely when hardly anything else feels safe. I admit that this life was more enjoyable when I lived it in the midst of other priests who shared my vision. The argument between my friends in the restaurant, now many months past, is just one example of how the once-common vision among priests has become fractured. No matter what happens to anybody else, however, I am still called—by name—by God, who loves me.

The Catholic priesthood in America now has a high profile, and that profile is mostly negative. Pedophilia, mismanagement of funds, broken celibacy promises, sexual orientation—all these topics and more are open targets in discussions, debates, and commentaries about priests. Clergy bashing takes place at almost any Catholic gathering—from adult education classes to baptism parties. We are paying the price of being placed on such a high pedestal up until a few years ago. And now we know the damage that has been done. The current headlines and media attention have shaped somewhat the purpose of this book, which is to remove any mystery or melodrama from people's perceptions of a priest's ministry and life. Neither hero nor saint, but also neither tragic loser nor addicted idealist, I am just an ordinary person who still finds incredible joy, profound awe, silencing mystery, and overwhelming peace as a priest.

So often, smack-dab in the middle of pain, God's grace burns right through. Those are the unpredictable moments I live for. They are what fill any priesthood with life and meaning. Those are the stories I want to tell. I need, in this day's tense and painful atmosphere, to celebrate my priesthood. I have a feeling that there are people who can benefit from reading the specific stories that create for me the meaning of this priestly calling.

So allow me to try to capture and present to you, with sincere humility, some of the events that have convinced me of how blessed my life has been and continues to be. In the pages that follow, let us listen together to God's call not only for me but for all of us.

Part One

Moments
That Matter

1

The Call Back

I realize that, for this moment in time, a person has come to me for my help. This encounter, perhaps our only one in history, reminds me that I am not here for me and my needs.

I T WAS A STRANGE VOICE MAIL, but then again, as a pastor I have grown accustomed to odd messages. Sounding very professional, the woman stated that her pastor had suggested she talk to me about the serious spiritual crisis in which she now found herself. She indicated that she would call me back to make an appointment; then she hung up without leaving her phone number. The next day she reached me and very coolly agreed to an afternoon meeting. I wondered why her pastor would refer her to me. That question would never be answered.

On the day of our appointment, she arrived at the rectory a half-hour early and walked into my office without hesitation. Fortunately I was free. She was informally but well dressed and could have passed for one of the thousands of young professionals I see in the neighborhood. I do not remember more than a sentence or two of initial pleasantries exchanged. She quickly got to the point. She wanted to know if I thought that God would punish her with hell if she committed suicide.

She must have noticed the confused look on my face as I tried to focus my thoughts and muster a response, because she volunteered to tell me her story. She then began a half-hour, nonstop account of how her family continued to abuse and harass her. She spoke vaguely of restraining orders, of physical fights with her sister, of her mother always taking her siblings' side and never hers. At times during this diatribe her anger would explode into shouts and questions: *How could they do this to her? What kind of people were they?*

I waited for the chance to speak. I have been a priest long enough to know that there is a point at which the best I can do for someone is refer him or her to a professional counselor. But I knew that this solution would be unacceptable to her—in her eyes I would be just another person ignoring her and pushing her off onto someone else. This was just what her pastor appeared to have done, unfortunately.

When I finally found an opportunity to speak, I asked her if she was taking any medications. She volunteered that none had been given to her when she left the psychiatric ward of a local hospital a few days prior to our meeting. She was vague about her departure. I suspected that she had chosen to check herself out.

When she started to repeat some of the same stories, I decided to interject with some advice. She had admitted that she functioned better when she was on medication, so I suggested that she go back to see the doctor she had rejected. There was no one else she could turn to. Her family was the focus and the cause of her anger, and in her mind, her friends had all deserted her. When I finally suggested that she talk to the professional pastoral counselor on our staff, she responded just as I feared she would. I had to tell her that yelling at me was unacceptable and would do neither of us any good. I tried to explain to her that the counselor would simply pick up where I left off and was trained to better help her, had more resources, and, as a woman, might better understand her. I added that the counseling was free of charge.

I'd hardly finished saying all of this when she resumed her ranting. Her anger toward me grew when I refused to be caught up in her argument about God abandoning her and then coldly condemning her to hell if she chose to kill herself. All I could do was keep repeating that she was not alone, that I was there for her, and that God loved her unconditionally. Finally, out of sheer frustration—and some surprise at the words I heard coming out of my mouth—I told her that if she chose to kill herself, it would not be God punishing her with hell; she would be making that choice for herself. She would have no one to blame but herself. Clearly this was not what she wanted to hear. She wanted the decision and the subsequent consequences taken out of her hands and given to God so that she could have even more reason to be angry with God.

Frustrated with me and still angry, she rose to leave. I remained seated. I continued to look her in the eyes. I told her again that God loved her. I told her that I cared about her and would be there for her. She tossed both comments off. I said that all that was left for me to do was to continue praying for her, and that I would do so every day. I would not let her stop me from doing that much.

She left. I followed her to the door and watched her walk down the gangway from the rectory to the church. I considered it highly probable that she would take her life. But I didn't know what more I could have done. I found myself walking right over to church to pray for her. I realized that she was already in the hell she feared so much; hell was her despair, emptiness, anger, and frustration. The tangle of mental illness combined with the deep spiritual despair that haunted her was beyond my skills to counsel and to heal. I too was feeling powerless and humbled. I was tempted to turn my prayers to my own needs, to obsess over what else I could have done. I knew that I must pray for her and leave her in God's loving hands. Yet I kept wondering what good, if any, I had done.

These are the situations that test my faith. My fallibility is placed right before me. I am dealing with a human life in pain and a soul in the profoundest struggle. Such encounters are haunting. They stay with me. *What else could I have said? What else should I have done? Why couldn't I find the right response? Maybe if I prayed more, worked harder at being the best priest I could be, wasn't so self-absorbed.* This is where my thinking goes. And I find my own faith being seriously tested.

I didn't wake up that day expecting someone to come into my office with her personal demons and challenge me so directly. Beyond the human response of wanting to respond to her anger with some of my own, there was also the feeling of having been violated. My comfortable world, my satisfying life, my fulfilling ministry, my sustaining belief system—all were attacked and questioned. She had raised all sorts of doubts that I thought I had buried for good a long time ago.

When confronted by a situation like this one, I have to respond. I can't just sit quietly and stare at the person. How do I proceed?

I realize that, for this moment in time, a person has come to me for my help. This encounter, perhaps our only one in history, reminds me that I am not here for me and my needs. I am here for someone else. This is both a privilege of the priesthood and a challenge. I'm not trying to be melodramatic. I simply take a deep breath and try to do the best I can. That's when God takes over. And that's when my own prayer becomes as real as it gets.

At morning Mass the day after I met with the troubled woman, I could not stop thinking about her. When I went back to my office and heard her voice on my voice mail, I was more than a little surprised. The message was brief and her tone matter-of-fact: she asked if I would please have our pastoral counselor give her a call. And she left a number. She had survived the night. There was still hope. As I filled the counselor in on what had happened, I wasn't concerned about whether or not I had responded in the right way. I was just thankful that God had found some way to work through me, or even in spite of me. In the end, it is God's unconditional love that causes transformation. I am grateful even to be included in the process.

2

Remembering Faces

If I make the effort to establish relationships with people, God will sometimes use those relationships in miraculous ways.

I ONCE KNEW A PRIEST who never forgot a name. He was a terrible administrator, a usually long-winded and pious preacher, and an often autocratic and abrupt pastor. But people loved him. In fact, some of them really saw him as a saint. They were blind to his faults. What was important to them was that he knew them by name and was able to recognize them week to week, even after years had passed.

That is an awesome gift for anyone to have, but it is especially useful for a priest for a number of reasons, the most important one being that a large part of the job is visiting with the congregation on the steps of the church before and after Mass. To be able to recognize a majority of the churchgoers by name is quite an accomplishment. And to still be able to call them by name having not seen them for years is nearly miraculous. Because we move from assignment to assignment, we priests have people coming in and out of our lives constantly. These people can easily remember us as their priests, while it is nearly impossible for us to remember them and from where we should know them. No wonder the priest with the uncanny ability to remember names became so special to so many people.

I, on the other hand, really struggle with names. Sometimes during the course of a meeting with someone, I forget the person's name. Once I tried to fake it while helping a couple fill out their wedding questionnaire. I had drawn a blank on the name of the bride, whom I had just met, and so I asked, "Spell your name for me, please, so I get the right variation." She hesitated and then smiled at me, saying sweetly but quizzically: "M-A-R-Y." Oh, well, it was a nice try.

Now when people come up to me wearing big smiles of recognition and say, "Father, remember me?" I do not even try to fake it. I just say, "The face is familiar. But please give me a name." Then all I have to do is hope that I can remember from where I should know them.

I try especially hard to remember those people I meet who I might be able to turn to when I am called on to assist people. A good priest has a network of contacts to assist him in his ministry. In such cases, I sometimes simply ask for a favor outright. Other times, and in a mysterious way, the right person just appears to be at the right place at the right time. In those moments it becomes very clear to me that I am partnering with God to do God's work and not my own. It is very humbling. But it doesn't just happen. I have to be doing my part.

I always make a point of getting to know the commander of the local police district. Commanders and police officers can really come in handy. Once I was able to save a former student of mine who became a police recruit from being let go by the department. I asked the local commander, whom I knew well, to intervene on a minor infraction that occurred out of state. Since he had a son who was roughly the same age as the recruit, the commander immediately understood and was happy to call his counterpart in Indiana to settle things. My former student is now an undercover police officer. Another time I requested that the commander talk to a group of seminarians visiting the city to learn more about urban ministry. He was pleased to do so, and it was a remarkably honest session.

Then there are those special, graced moments when God puts it all together beyond my wildest expectations. It is then that I know why it is so important to be building relationships with God's people.

A few years ago I received a message from a public defender. He had taken over a case just in time for the sentencing. The young man he was defending had been found guilty and was facing a term in the state prison. Unfortunately, he was mentally challenged—not enough, in the court's eyes, to be inculpable, but enough that imprisonment in the state penitentiary would destroy him. The public defender was grasping at straws. Since the young man had helped out at parish events, would I come and plead his case to the judge before the sentencing?

I arrived at court to find a nervous public defender. He was just out of law school, and this was his first case. The young man, not aware of his fate, waved excitedly to me. He was oblivious of everything. When the judge walked in, I immediately recognized him as the father of one of my former students in the seminary. When asked if I could be permitted to speak, he gave me permission, speaking of his respect for me and for all the work I had done with his son. He implied that he would take whatever I recommended very seriously into account.

So I suggested that the young man, though already found guilty, be put on probation and released into the custody of his mother. The judge concurred. He then turned to the probation officer and asked for his opinion. The probation officer and I smiled at each other. It seemed that he was one of my former students as well. He also agreed without any reservations, citing that he too knew me and trusted my judgment.

The young man was released to his mother and has not been in trouble since. The public defender was incredulous, asking me if everybody in the court system knew who I was. I simply smiled and told him no, just the ones who needed to today. The irony is that outside of that courtroom I probably would not have recognized either the judge or the probation officer if they had come up to me and said, "Father, remember me?" But through the grace of God they were at the right place at the right time, and so I was able to do the right thing. I will continue to learn new names and forget others. I still can be found on the church steps every Sunday, making contacts and developing relationships that will come in handy when God decides to use them.

3

Weddings I Have Known and Loved

I want the couple to believe that the love God has chosen to give them can, if they let nothing else get in the way of it, take them through the doors of death and into eternity together.

ILIKE WEDDINGS. You won't find too many priests who feel this way, certainly not those who celebrate close to eighty weddings a year, as I have been doing. Before I go any further, let me make it clear that I adamantly do not like wedding rehearsals. And I will refrain from sharing with you my feelings about those paid wedding coordinators, most of whom can claim Amazon terrorists in their lineage—and this includes the guys.

I like weddings. That means, for sake of clarification, that I like it from the moment the prelude music stops and I say, "Please stand." At that point the trumpet and organ, occasionally at the same time, begin the march of the bridesmaids, who wear dresses they would otherwise never be caught dead in.

You must appreciate that to get to this moment, I have to survive a veritable crossfire of florists, photographers, mothers of the bride and groom, flower girls, ring bearers, and groomsmen. And surviving often proves to be a difficult task.

Florists will use the stickiest tape invented, yet the paper runner on the aisle will not stay in place. But the tape does stay stuck to the church floor, usually for decades. Some florists do not quite understand that the thousand-dollar spray of flowers they want to set proudly in the middle of the altar will make my celebrating Mass a real challenge. And if you don't treat them nicely, they slow down and make sure the ceremony starts even later than usual.

Photographers fall into two categories: the still and the video. Ninety-five percent of still photographers are professionals just trying to make an honest dollar, or ten thousand. For some reason unknown to me, it's the opposite for the videographers. I think maybe this is because they are frustrated Steven Spielbergs.

My favorite still shot from any wedding is a composite, with the groom looking into his champagne glass at his new bride, who is therein, peering back at him. Unfortunately the groom is looking into the glass as if there is a bug in his drink and the bride looks as if she is drowning. The couple wouldn't let me order that one from the proofs. One photographer actually tried to stand in the celebrant's chair behind me to get a good shot over my shoulder. And this was after he was told specifically not to go up on the altar area. A videographer once requested that I move out of his way so he could get a better shot of the couple's exchange of vows.

I could go on about photographers. I won't.

Then there was the mother of the bride who insisted on holding up the wedding for an hour so that a cab could bring her the corsage she'd left at the hotel. Finally, we gave her Grandma's corsage and gave Grandma the "surprise" rose (a more recent tradition) Mom never would get—or miss, for that matter—at the sign of peace. Flower girls have been known to eat the rose petals while walking down the aisle, and more than one ring bearer has swallowed the ring or lost the pillow. How wonderfully human it all becomes.

I like weddings. What kind of crazed masochist am I, you might be asking, to like this sort of stuff two or three times a Saturday? I'll explain. I love seeing the couple at the moment they touch hands after the bride's long walk down the aisle. No matter how sophisticated they try to be, there is usually a tentativeness and a simplicity about them at this moment that makes it magical, even if they do not recognize it themselves.

The grooms and the brides are not always the ideals I would like them to be. One bride decided that once she put on her white dress she would not take it off for any reason until her wedding day was over. No trips to the bathroom for her. She stopped drinking and eating more than twenty-four hours before the ceremony. Not surprisingly, right after coming down the aisle she passed out into a cloud of billowing white silk and satin from which the paramedic had to cut her. Another time I had to fight distraction all the way through my homily because the groom looked at his watch eleven times as I preached. What was the problem? Did he leave the meter running or have another appointment? At least he didn't lock himself in the can and refuse to come out, as did another groom, struck with mortal fear.

No matter what else happens, it is my homily that I try to protect and that I find to be so important. Somehow I want the couple to believe with all their hearts that the love God has chosen to give them to share with each other—and with family, friends, the poor and the lost, and God as well—is so incredibly powerful and mysterious that if they let nothing else get in the way of it, it can and will take them through the doors of death and into eternity together. If I sense that they really have heard me, I've done my job.

And, believe it or not, this message can be communicated despite the groom who wants his dog to be his best man and despite Uncle Louie standing on a pew to get the best shot with his new camcorder and despite the bride's dad stepping on her veil, causing the phony hair attached to it to fly across the altar, and despite the unity candle refusing to stay lit and despite Aunt Lucy sounding like Cher on steroids as she attempts to sing "Ave Maria."

I like weddings. After I give the final blessing and introduce the couple to the applause and whistles of the congregation, they walk out to a triumphant march, taking what I call "the victory lap." It is often at that moment that I find myself engulfed in silence, deep in thought, wondering what their futures will hold. Will they ever be any happier than they are at this moment? For my part, I have tried to give them the best shot of God's grace and love that I could despite all those externals whipping around us. Their lives, their hopes, and their trust are such a mystery. I am left with nothing else to say . . . that is, until the photographer starts to dismantle everything on the altar for the sake of the pictures.

As I said, I like weddings.

4

Liturgy for One

I may celebrate Mass hundreds of times, but each time I have to act as if this is the most important Mass I will ever celebrate.

HELPING OUT AT A PARISH on weekends is far different from being the pastor of that parish. I've done both. You develop deeper relationships when you're pastor, moving around and among the people of the church, but the responsibilities and stresses can be greater. By the same token, when all you do is come in and celebrate Mass, you don't develop the same relationships, but you are free of the headaches that come with pastoral responsibilities and decision making.

Years ago, I was helping out at St. Germaine Parish, celebrating Mass and filling in as the pastor needed me.

One Sunday morning I arrived late at the parish. The suburb's annual marathon had succeeded in blocking every conceivable route to the church. I ran into the sacristy with a scant few minutes to spare before Mass was supposed to begin. The congregation evidently was also having trouble getting to the church. It was almost empty.

Not surprisingly, I was distracted, angry, and feeling as though I had no message to communicate in my homily. I made a quick decision to just get through the Mass. However, as the opening hymn concluded, I could not help but notice a young woman in the very first pew. How sad and troubled she looked. How deep in the struggle of prayer she seemed to be. I knew at that moment that I would have to celebrate the best Mass I could for her and try to say something in my homily that would make a difference in her life. As the service proceeded, I couldn't tell what kind of impact my words were having on her. But I did end Mass satisfied, feeling that I had given her and the rest of the congregation my best effort.

This could have been one of those countless nondescript moments of ministry that would fade away over the years. But it came back to me in a surprising way long after the moment had passed and my ministry had taken me across the diocese.

I had applied for and been named pastor of a struggling urban parish, its potential still very well hidden. So I was graciously invited by the pastor at St. Germaine to say farewell to the congregation at all the Masses. This goodbye was scheduled for Father's Day weekend, but I did not want my departure to take away from the holiday, which I felt would be foremost in the minds of the parishioners. So we compromised, the pastor insisting that people needed to say their goodbyes. I would celebrate and say farewell at the last scheduled liturgy, and a brief reception would follow for any who wanted to attend.

I was surprised by the size of the crowd in the church and even more so by the number of parishioners who used up some of their Father's Day to stand in line in the hall after Mass. There were lots of embraces, kisses, and envelopes, all more than I had expected. I drove home thanking God for the experience that weekends at that parish had been for me.

My first two weeks as pastor in the new parish were extremely rocky. I did not expect that some of the old-time parishioners would want to test me so much. There were lots of surprises, precious little warmth, and innumerable rumors flying through the air. On my third Sunday afternoon there, after three unrewarding liturgies (especially unrewarding when compared to my recent experience at St. Germaine), it started to rain. I sat on a ledge in my room in the rectory and looked out at the gray storm. It seemed as good a time as any to open the cards I had received from the people at St. Germaine. I really needed some reassurance.

The very first card I opened contained a note. I did not recognize the name signed at the bottom. In the note a woman thanked me for my years helping out at St. Germaine Parish. She wished me well as the new pastor of St. Josaphat. She was certain that I would have success there. And then she told me why.

She acknowledged that I probably would not know who she was or remember a particular Sunday morning some time ago when she sat in the first pew. She described how difficult it was for her to pray that day and how mightily she was struggling to find God. But during my homily she felt as though I were celebrating Mass just for her. The words of my homily brought her much peace and a sense of God's unconditional love for her. She thanked me for that special Mass and assured me that I would reach the people of my new parish in the same way.

The memory of that Sunday years before came flooding back. Obviously, I have no way of knowing if this woman who wrote me was indeed the woman in the first pew to whom I had dedicated my Mass. But I do choose to believe that they are one and the same person and that God used her to tell me that everything would be okay in the new parish.

Was it her or not? It's a wonderful mystery that will never be solved. And neither will the mystery of why God continues to work through me to minister to others and then in turn ministers even more to me, through these same people.

When I stop to think of all the Masses I have celebrated over the years—on weekends and during the week, at weddings, funerals, retreats, and other times—and all those people who shared in those liturgies, I am overwhelmed. How has God used me in people's lives at this very apex of prayer? How will I ever know? "Nice Mass, Father" is usually all I hear.

Notes such as the one from that mysterious woman come every once in a while and always unexpectedly. They are meant to be savored, to be read over again, especially at those times when I'm just not sure if what I am doing makes any difference. These notes tell me that I am. Let this be my thanks to all who have written them over the years.

5

Talking to the Priest

Sometimes I can't offer much, just an
invitation to others to have a little more faith.

ONE OF THE TASKS I perform regularly is
being there when someone needs to "talk to a
priest." You can never predict what these conversations will be about. So usually as I am welcoming
the person into my office, I am also saying a little prayer
that I can be helpful, whatever his or her need may be.

One such situation sticks out in my mind. I received a
call early one morning from a young man who identified
himself as a parishioner. I did not recognize his name.
Could he come and talk with me about an issue of faith
in his life? I assured him that he could. Could it be
tomorrow? Could it be tomorrow before 9:00 A.M.? He

and his wife and child were leaving to go on vacation somewhere in the Southern Hemisphere.

So the next morning, promptly at 8:00 A.M., he walked into my office. No one could better fit the look and the temperament of the type-A young folks moving into the gentrified neighborhood. I am lousy at reading people accurately at first sight. So I tried hard not to set any judgment on him before he told his story.

I was surprised and moved by what he told me. He had been married for fourteen years and had known his wife for four years prior to their marriage. In those years before they got married, she had gotten pregnant and they had mutually made the decision to have an abortion. Though their decision still haunted him, he knew he had been wrong and had confessed it. After he and his wife were married they found themselves unable to conceive again. They went to a specialist for lengthy treatments but were given little hope. So they eventually stopped trying and planned on adopting. They were more than pleasantly surprised when they suddenly found themselves pregnant. They became the parents of a healthy child.

Throughout all that happened, this man never lost faith in God's love for him. He told me that he never felt that God was punishing them for what they had done. He felt that he had worked out a better relationship with God because of all that had happened and because of the choices they had made way back then. He felt forgiven, but challenged, he said.

The problem he was coming to talk to me about was something new. His wife's biological clock was ticking.

She wanted another child, and that would mean going back to the doctor and starting a whole new series of tests, followed by treatments and examinations. He was hesitant to restart the process, but he also knew that this was putting a terrible strain on his relationship with his wife. With an extended vacation ahead of them, he was desperate to figure out what to do.

Here stood a man used to being able to find answers to his problems, a take-charge kind of guy now dealing with a growing sense of hopelessness but still trying to find the right thing to do. My heart went out to him as I felt my own lack of children, due to my own life choices.

He offered to tell me why the decision was such a struggle for him this time. While he believed that God had not been punishing him for his prior actions, he did feel guilty about how he had taken the "natural and sacred mystery of life," as he called it, into his own hands. He felt that this was why he and his wife had not conceived. And it was only when he insisted that they stop the treatments that life took its natural and there-fore sacred course. But now time was literally running out. He looked at me and said softly, "Father, help me figure out what God wants me to do."

All of a sudden I found myself in the place where I feel the least comfortable: a parishioner's bedroom. The church's teaching on human sexuality can be both beau-tiful and cruel. Human sexuality is a mystery that defies science, be that the science of human reproduction or the science that is theology. I believe that we could study human sexuality from now until Gabriel blows the trumpet and it would still remain the exquisite mystery that God made it to be.

Some priests ignore these issues because they are inherently volatile. Some priests—with astonishing assuredness—communicate the party line, the official church rules and explanations. I tend to bow before the mystery. God will be with two people who prayerfully choose, after hearing all the options, to do what they honestly feel is the loving action. So I will not allow myself to become judge or jury or obstetrician or therapist.

As a priest I communicate God's love for his people— and the obligation that this love brings—and then I pray with and for those who have come to me. The rest is between them and God.

Some may criticize me for this approach, claiming that it's too easy on people. But my experiences in these situations have convinced me that leaving the final decision up to the people involved makes the strongest demands on them. And most people respond to these demands nobly and heroically.

Early in my priesthood I learned that it is better to help people come to an insight or at least find the courage and strength to face their battles more confidently than it is to just give someone advice. But this man's newfound vulnerability moved me to tell him just what I was feeling.

I suggested to him that since the child he loved so dearly came a full two years after he and his wife stopped going to doctors, and since his wife, frightened and anxious, felt the need to try the tests again, he should be open to both realities. He looked at me quizzically. I had not done a good job of making myself clear. So I got even more direct. I didn't plan my words; they just came out.

I told him that he should go to the doctors with his wife and take whatever tests they gave him. Then, before receiving any of the results, he and his wife should make love. Since both of their previous conceptions had occurred naturally, they would be showing their faith that it could happen again. The mystery of the natural flow of life would still be there even if the test results showed that conceiving would be impossible or remotely possible. I knew I was setting him up for some difficult discussions with his wife if they did not conceive and if the test results came back with hard news. But we would be able to talk again. I wished I could say more. I invited him to share my suggestion with his wife.

I received a phone call a few weeks later. I don't know if it came from Brazil, an airport, or down the block. Things were better between him and his wife. They were putting their trust in God no matter what happened. I hadn't offered them much, just an invitation to have a little more faith. I gave them no guarantees. I had not been judgmental. Maybe that, more than anything I had said, was what allowed God's grace to work.

6

"Tell Me What to Do"

At the point of death, it is not the spouse or child but the priest who is asked the most critical questions and trusted for the most important answers.

SOMETIMES MY ONLY POINT of entry into people's lives is the doorway opened by the reality and mystery of death. Over the years I have learned to respect death. Embraced or repulsed, death comes when it chooses to come, often well before the last breath is taken. It is an awesome mystery.

I got to know one family in particular through death, the uninvited guest that would not leave their home. A vibrant woman with a devoted husband and loving son fought a brain tumor with all her will. In desperation, her family invited me to visit her and to pray with her. We hit it off immediately. When the family told me that my visits seemed to relieve her, at least for a while, of the tremendous pain she was enduring, I insisted that the family call me the minute the medication stopped working and they felt that she needed me.

She was not Catholic, but when she died, her funeral in the Catholic Church celebrated a faith in the Resurrection as strong as any I have ever experienced. Unfortunately, that faith could never soften the loss that the husband and son felt. They would get along somehow and eventually begin to live their lives again, lives that had been put on hold because of her illness and dying, but they would always be aware of her absence.

The husband's parents were solid as rocks, possessing that old-country style of faith that simply accepts death as very much a part of life. Despite their years and their own failing health, they were tremendous supports for their son and grandson. When I received a phone call to come to the hospital because both of them were seriously ill, I knew that I would once again be drawn into the life of this family, and that I would once again confront with them their nemesis, death.

The grandfather was the more gravely ill of the two, already on life support when I arrived and with nothing positive in his prognosis. His wife was far off in another wing of the hospital. She was fighting stomach cancer. She would eventually be allowed to go home, but for how long no one seemed willing to predict.

I brought the blessed oil and the holy water with which I would anoint them both. The son and grandson were resigned to the reality that their father and grandfather would not be leaving the hospital alive. So they prayed with me and cried with me. After consultations with the doctors, it became painfully clear that the family would have to ask the man's wife for permission to take him off life support. The doctors were certain that without it he would not live through the night. The family looked to me for support. Could I go with them, anoint Grandmother, and then somehow help them help her reach what would be a heart-wrenching decision—a decision no one ever wants to make, but especially difficult for a woman already wracked by illness herself.

When we arrived at her room we tried to put off talking about her husband until we had ministered to her. But she knew something was wrong. I blessed her, anointing her with the oils on her forehead and hands, and then sprinkled her with the holy water. She wanted me to sit next to her on the bed. We all knew that the time had come.

We went into our rehearsed scripts. The doctor began by explaining to her the gravity of her husband's condition. Then her son gently restated the doctor's words so that there would be no confusion or false hope of recovery to complicate the situation. I went next, reassuring her that I had anointed her husband and that he truly seemed to be at peace and less restless after all the prayers had been said.

How unfair life is when such a difficult decision is left to one so feeble and small and vulnerable. But her appearance belied a genuine strength that grew out of the long years she and her husband had spent together and their unshakable, shared belief in the God who loved them.

After listening to all of us she first asked the doctor what she would do. The doctor, with great compassion, took her hand and caressed it, saying that if it were her father she would make the decision to take him off life support so that his suffering could come to an end. After a brief pause, the woman looked at her son and asked him what he would do. Crying, the son assured his mother that there was nothing more the doctors could do and that it was the only logical and right choice, no matter how difficult it would be to make. His mother took some time to digest his words.

Then she reached over to the corner of the bed upon which I was still sitting and took my hand. I could still feel the oil I had placed on her hand just moments earlier. In retrospect, it was as if she were now anointing me. She looked at me. She didn't ask me what I would do, as she had asked the doctor and her son. With amazing confidence and faith, she said, "Father, you tell me now what to do." With our hands still joined, I emphasized that I could not tell her what to do. But I told her that I did support the doctor and her son and suggested that she should have her husband taken from the machines so that God would be allowed to do whatever God felt was best. She agreed to turn off the machines. And since she was confined to her bed and could not see him before it happened, she asked if I would stay with him until the end. I assured her that I would.

As it turned out, when the machines were turned off, her husband rallied, surprising everyone. After he made it through the night, the family decided to place him in hospice care. I could go home. But before I did, I asked the doctor to allow the man's faith-filled wife to visit her husband one final time so that she could kiss him good-bye, pray over him, and see that she had indeed made the right decision. It appeared that God had decided to give him enough time so that she could say farewell.

I admired this woman's strong faith. But I couldn't help coming back to the fact that the doctor, and even her son, were asked only for their suggestions. For whatever reason, it was left to me, the priest, to tell her what to do. Even now, remembering the weight that my suggestions carried, I am left speechless and humbled.

7

Passion and the Priesthood

The love that draws people to God is passionate and fully engaged.

THE WORDS *PASSION* AND *PRIEST* don't seem to fit comfortably side by side. Think about the images of priests you encounter in books, on TV, or at the movies. The on-fire, deeply passionate, loving priest usually leaves the ministry by the time the story has unfolded.

After showing a film on the priesthood back when I taught at the high school seminary, I was struck by the way a woman in the film described the parish priest: "He always looks like he's sucking on lemons." How sad! How often this becomes the image stuck in people's minds.

Well, it's not the case with me. When I laugh, it is out loud. I cry often. I'm quick to anger. And I love deeply. The only priesthood I know is one filled with passion. It does wear me out. It might even shorten my life span. But it is only by being passionate that I can be the effective priest I have to be. I've continued to learn and relearn this over the years.

My memories are themselves lessons. Here are some freeze-frames of experiences that have shaped me. They all have to do with passionate love.

Frame one: I am in seminary. These are turbulent times for the country and the church. It is the era of the late sixties and early seventies, when many structures and paradigms that have been so solid are beginning to crumble and be tossed aside. I am listening to a priest on the faculty give a stirring talk, challenging parish priests to become revolutionaries. Unfortunately, that same priest leaves the priesthood the following week to marry one of the nuns who has been brought in to teach us. We aren't that upset or surprised. Such departures are regular occurrences during these times. It seems that, so often, passion takes people away from the traditional church structures.

Frame two: A pastor of a small inner-city church is speaking to us seminarians. He tells us that he leaves the front door of his church wide open while he celebrates morning Mass so that he can include in the sparse congregation all the people who disinterestedly walk past the doors. The point he is so desperately trying to make to us is that to be effective in our ministry we have to fall in love—and stay in love—with the people of God whom we are allowed to serve, even when they do not love us in return.

Frame three: As I am driving my last carload of possessions to my new rectory residence, I am forced to pull over to the side of the road because, thinking about the people I'm leaving behind, I begin to cry and cannot stop the tears. I have been reassigned to teach after only one year in the parish. I don't know, on this bleak day, that I will thoroughly enjoy my thirteen years of teaching. But in my heart I do know that I am a parish priest. The natural flow of high school students and their families over a four-year time span will never allow for the same level of ministry and, therefore, for the same type of relationships to evolve.

Frame four: I am sitting with a group of priests, talking about relationships with parishioners. A remarkable preacher and speaker, a man whose charisma dramatically draws crowds, says that he can best minister to people by distancing himself from them. It takes too much energy to love them, he says. Not long after that discussion, he leaves the priesthood. He tries a few times to return on a part-time basis, unable to make that important commitment. Not surprisingly, it does not work.

Frame five: I am eavesdropping on an elderly couple at dinner in a restaurant. They talk animatedly with each other, and it is clear that they have spent most of their lives together. But they are still discovering each other. That allows for comfort and peacefulness to encompass them. I learn a lesson about relationships.

The first book I wrote came about when I had returned to parish ministry full-time. Interestingly, its title is *Do You Love Me?* By then, I was beginning to understand the depth of love that is required of priests—and, indeed, of anyone—who want to live God's kingdom on this earth.

My fifteen years as a pastor have affected the way I look at my ministry and at who I am. I realize now that I am most fully a priest when I am in relationship—more specifically, in loving relationship—with the people of God. And like most loving relationships, it is never complete or final but always in a state of growth, of change, of renewal. Together we are a work in progress and can remain so only if we realize how graced we are by the God who has brought us together.

Over the years my relationship with these people has truly grown into a relationship of passionate love. Their hopes, their joys, and their fears have become mine. Our stories are intertwined. They know me, warts and all, and yet love me. And this motivates me to empower them to find their own call to share in the priesthood of Jesus Christ.

It is precisely in that common vocation, in that place where our souls touch—in those exquisite expressions of love, be they liturgical, sacramental, personal, or spiritual—that we become the church together. It is in that intimacy that my priesthood is fulfilled and blossoms. And together we are graced by God. Although our love will never be perfect or finished, I believe that it has achieved a certain quality that is possible only after years together—in the same way that love between a husband and a wife develops out of time and trust and trying and failing.

My relationship with my parishioners is moving inexorably to that place—although this is a pilgrim journey and therefore never finished. I am with them now not because of any title of priest or pastor but because of the person I am. They know my strengths and my many limitations. At the same time, their sharing more of themselves with me allows me to see all the good that is in them. And as we continue to discover one another, our love grows.

I treasure my memories of those times when this love is revealed in momentous ways, such as when I celebrated my twenty-fifth anniversary as a priest and the day we rededicated our restored church. But I also cherish the simple message in the e-mail thanking me for a particular homily, or the note sent for no particular reason, or the swiftness to say yes to being part of a program, or sharing a reflection, or joining a committee. I could go on and on. But I will say only that I have fallen in love and will continue to be in love as long as I am able to minister to these wonderful people. For me, passion and priesthood are one and the same.

8

"Is That All?"

Patient parents may help form a priest, but that doesn't mean a priest's parents can't try his patience.

ITALIANS AND SOME other nationalities share the belief that a priest's mother automatically earns heaven. On the surface this seems quaintly pious. Consider it again. It just may be saying something about a priest's temperament and a mother's patience. I'm not sure.

In any case my mother took that belief quite seriously. I am not sure exactly when it happened, but a few years before my ordination, when she was sufficiently certain that I was going to do it, she stopped wearing her wedding diamond. She did not want to risk losing it. You see, another Italian custom is that the mother's diamond ring is set into the newly ordained priest's chalice. And this is where Mom's ring rests today, thanks to my brother, who designed and cast my chalice.

The irony of this is that when Mom turned seventy-five, many years after my ordination, it became my task to ask my father to buy his wife the new diamond ring she had picked out for her birthday present. At the time, he could no longer speak because of a series of strokes he had suffered, but I remember his eyebrows rising up into his forehead after I told him the cost of the ring.

I know my parents were proud of me, but it was partly misdirected pride of my vocation ("There aren't too many who are priests!"), which often drove me crazy. At the same time, my dad, God rest his soul, could never fully figure out how I was earning an honest living on a priest's salary. In any case, their pride was blended with their feeling that a priest in the family could prove to be very useful. This combination tested my sense of humor as well as my humility and patience.

I was thus tested one particular summer day when my parents set up a house blessing for me to celebrate. It would be no ordinary blessing of a house. I would be blessing my aunt and uncle's new condominium. My aunt was Mom's sister and my uncle was Dad's brother. Not only that, but my aunt and uncle were also my godparents. Ours was a close-knit family. They had moved from a beautiful house that had become too large for them to care for into a fashionable high rise on the downtown

Chicago lakefront. They would be living in the same building as their son, my cousin.

When I arrived to do the house blessing, I was given a tour of their second-floor apartment. That went pretty quickly, but not so quickly that I couldn't appreciate their beautiful view of Lake Michigan. After the tour, I spent some time trying to help my uncle understand that the cable stations on his television in the new house were not the same as those he had been used to in his old house. I wasn't sure if he was following me or not, but then my mother announced grandly that it was time for me to bless the house.

So, obedient son that I was, I took out my book of blessings and led us all in prayer. I then took my flask of holy water and went from room to room in the apartment, blessing each one of them. I sincerely tried to do a good job. You can imagine my surprise, then, when Mom took me aside after I finished and, in a not-too-subtle whisper, asked, "Is that all?"

In my mind, it was; I had performed the standard house blessing. When I questioned Mom about what else I should have or could have done, she could not come up with anything. But it was much too short and perfunctory a blessing for her liking. I was utterly embarrassed when she told me to figure out something else to do. Even though my aunt and uncle seemed pleased and coffee was being poured, I knew that I had to come up with something, and pretty quickly.

My pride was hurt, and I was more than a little angry. I decided that if Mom wanted more, then by God, she would get more. Without saying a word, I ushered all four of them out the door of the apartment. When we got to the elevator, I pressed the up button and took us all the way—more than fifty floors—to the top floor. When the elevator doors opened, I did not let the befuddled quartet exit. I simply took the holy water and sprinkled through the open doors. I then pressed every button down to two, lighting up the whole panel. At every floor on the way down, when the door opened, I sprinkled and blessed. If someone was waiting to board, it made no difference. They could be Catholic, Protestant, Hindu, Jewish, or atheist—they got the holy water if they didn't move aside quickly enough. I did all this without any explanation. All I said as the doors opened was "Bless the thirty-ninth floor" or "Bless the twenty-seventh floor." By the time we were back down on two I was totally satisfied that I had made my point.

When my aunt went to the kitchen to reheat the coffee, Mom turned to me with a look of both triumph and ecstasy. What a good son I was, she told me. That was an absolutely perfect blessing and no one could have done any better. Even Dad was beaming in appreciation. My sarcasm was lost completely on my proud parents.

My aunt and uncle are now deceased. But still, every time I drive past Harbor Point Towers when I am on Lake Shore Drive, I chuckle. The residents there don't know how blessed their building is. Fortunately, I know how blessed and challenging my priesthood has been with parents such as mine.

9

Hospital Visits Remembered—and Forgotten

It is too easy for me as a priest to lose track of moments of grace, to forget events that have been life changing for others but simple routine for me.

THERE IS A COMPULSIVE SIDE to me and a self-pitying side as well. Both appear especially when I am very tired. I start recounting how many couples I have married or how many baptisms I have celebrated. Then I start wishing I had more time for myself. Unfortunately, some of today's so-called timesaving devices record numbers for you. The worst of them for me is voice mail, which registers how many telephone messages I have received. If I have been away for even part of the day, the number I return to can be really overwhelming.

After listening to so many messages year after year, I can tell only two or three words into a message what the call is about. If the voice is not at all recognizable, there is a good chance the person is inquiring about a wedding date or a time for a baptism. Friends usually apologize for leaving a message. Sales folks sound much too cheerful. And parishioners with complaints, well, they have a tone all their own.

Recently I retrieved a message from a young woman who had called to ask me to drive to a Catholic hospital well across the city to anoint her grandmother before she was placed in hospice care. I did not recognize the name of the young woman, nor that of her failing grandmother. Nonetheless, I returned her call right away. She seemed thrilled to hear my voice. She told me that she would be at the hospital all day the next day getting her grandmother ready for the move to the hospice. What time would I be coming? Mentally shuffling a few appointments, I let her know approximately when I would get there.

As I was making the more than hourlong trip the following day, I kept asking myself how I had gotten roped into this task. While I could never begrudge anyone an anointing, especially not someone who was dying, I wondered how this young woman had convinced me to come to a Catholic hospital—which had chaplains on duty twenty-four hours a day—when she wasn't even a member of my parish. I kept thinking of all the other things I could have been doing with my time. As to be expected, traffic was not cooperating either. I was definitely going to be late for my meeting at the rectory, scheduled for when I returned from the hospital. Of course, the hospital's main parking lot was full. It was a long walk from the auxiliary lot to the main entrance (and priestly black suits aren't meant to be worn while walking in the sun on a hot day). By now the self-pity was kicking into high gear.

When I entered the patient's room, a young lady ran up to me, hugged me, and said with tears in her eyes that she knew I would come and now I would make everything all right, just as I had ten years ago. I didn't recognize her, and I had no idea what she referring to. Lucky for me, she volunteered her story. Ten years ago, she had called her pastor (she was from a neighboring parish) to come and baptize her child, who was in the emergency room of the Masonic hospital a few blocks away from her parish. Being a Masonic hospital, it had no chaplains on staff or on call. Unbelievably, the pastor told her that, as a recent arrival to the city, he did not know where the hospital was located, and asked if she could call back in a few hours when the associate pastor would be available. Instead she decided to call me. Evidently I arrived before her child died and was able to baptize and bless the baby. She never forgot my prompt arrival and my blessing of her child. And now she was overjoyed because I would bless her grandmother before she died as well. Grandmother never did wake up. I don't know if she was able to hear me, but I gave her a heartfelt anointing because I felt so bad for all that I had been thinking as I drove to the hospital.

Part of me was feeling guilty. Another part of me was deeply humbled. There I was, mumbling about losing a few minutes of my day, not knowing what a powerful impact I had made on this young woman—so powerful that she remembered me all these years later.

It is too easy for me as a priest to lose track of these special moments of grace, these truly sacramental moments when I am privileged to be a conduit of God's love for faith-filled people. These moments are why I am so blessed. That anointing that I found myself performing somehow became an awesome opportunity for grace, not only for the grandmother on her deathbed and for her loving granddaughter, but in a wonderful way for me as well. I was gently reminded of how important and lasting the work of my priesthood has been in the lives of so many people, even if I can't remember the details. This will bring me peace the next time I am called to yet another priestly duty and start to wonder why.

10

Permission to Die

Giving people permission to die has become a crucial part of my ministry.

MY FATHER TAUGHT ME many things, despite the fact that he was a man of few words. Some of what he taught me was how not to do what he had done. But he also gave me some very important lessons in life and death. One of his last lessons—and an awesome, mysterious one it was—took place the week before he died.

Because he had suffered a number of strokes, he could not speak. But he didn't have to. His pain was evident all over his body, a shell ready to crack one final time. Mom, sensing Dad's unease, asked me to come home and anoint him a last time. When I walked into the bedroom, which for six months had been the extent of his shrunken world, I was amazed to see him struggle and then lift himself out of his chair. I was saddened, embarrassed, even confused seeing the once-strong man who was my father stand there in a diaper. I realized that he was trying to show me that he was okay. He dreaded going to the hospital. He thought that was why I was there. So he stood to show me how strong he still was.

I gently sat him down. As I was getting the oils ready, I saw the fear in his eyes, and I knew I could not continue with the anointing. I put everything down and took his hand. In a soft voice I told him that he was going to die and that it was going to be soon. I couldn't believe what I heard myself saying. But I went on nonetheless. I told him that it was okay to be afraid. But I wanted him to know that it was also okay to let go and to die. I told him that his sons, all four of us, would watch out for Mom and that he had done a great job of providing for her. She would be taken care of. He seemed to relax a little, so I went on. I told him that we would all miss him and would be sad when he was gone, but we would be happy knowing that he was with his daughter, whom he loved so dearly and whose death had haunted him all his life. I mentioned his parents, the grandparents I had never met. Where were these words coming from?

He started to cry. But it wasn't one of the long sobbing spells that his strokes brought on. It was just a brief moment of cleansing, allowing his resignation to slowly melt into peace. Now was the moment. I gently anointed his head and his hands with the oil. Mom was crying softly. So was I. Dad died later that week, peacefully.

I prayed long and hard over that final encounter between Dad and me. I knew that it was a blessing for me both as his son and as a priest. But I wondered if I had ministered more to myself that to him.

Dad would help me answer that question more than once. Giving people permission to die has become a crucial part of my ministry as a priest. The opportunity has arisen a number of times. Sometimes I say something and other times I remain silent. I think of those final moments with Dad and then I am guided in the right direction.

I've given people permission to die when I was angry. A parishioner in denial of his terminal cancer refused to let his wife deal with it. He would not allow her to pray for him or comfort him; nor would he allow me to anoint him. When I saw how much pain he was causing her, I went into his bedroom and told him how selfish he was being. She needed to mourn with him because he would be dead in a few days even if he wouldn't admit it. What he did with this was up to him. I then left the room and told his wife what I had said. While we were talking he called us back into the room to pray with him. I told him he could now let go in peace. I returned to the rectory, and when I walked in the door, the phone was ringing. It was his wife. After I had left, he had kissed her and taken his last breath.

Another time I visited a man whose family I knew well. They often had me over for dinner. It was a close-knit family: Mom had died suddenly, and Dad enjoyed nothing more than having his family around him. Now he was dying. His children had asked me to come and talk with him. They all sensed that he was struggling when he should have been at peace. He smiled when I walked into the bedroom, but his face quickly clouded over as he talked about his illness. I chanced an observation. Was he feeling guilty for leaving his children alone? He burst into tears. I waited patiently and then had him talk about each one of his children and how well each was doing. I helped him to see that it was okay to die now because he had done a wonderful job as a father. Then I had the children come in one at a time to share a private moment with him. When I left, they were all together with him in the bedroom, and he had a peaceful smile on his face. He died just a few days later.

I remember looking down on my brother when he was on a respirator. At that moment I had power of attorney, I was his baby brother, and I was the priest who had just anointed him. As the one with power of attorney I did not let them remove the respirator. As his brother I told him how much I loved him. And as a priest I anointed him and prayed that he be restored to full health. I never thought of telling him to let go. When the doctor removed the respirator later, my brother started to breathe on his own and ultimately pulled through. There are times . . . and there are times.

In my heart I know that my presence at each death I've witnessed was not a coincidence. For whatever reason, my words were needed for that person's passage, whether it was a passage to death or to more life. Those sacramental moments keep me humble while reaffirming the Resurrection gospel that I am called to preach, believe, and live out in my ministry.

Less than a week after I wrote the first part of this reflection, I had to rush to the hospital to anoint a parishioner. Another priest had already gone there to anoint her while the staff attempted to locate me. But that priest did not know her or her family. Her children felt that she would want me there even though she had slipped out of consciousness. When I arrived I blessed her and talked to her. I told her that it was okay for her to let go and to be with her husband in heaven. The nurse was watching the monitor and came in a minute or two later, after I said goodbye to the family. As I turned to walk out of the ICU the nurse said simply, "She's gone, Father." The woman's son looked at me and said, "When you are having a bad day and doubt what you are doing, remember this. What incredible power you have." Then he went and kissed his mother.

Those times when I have helped people take that final step, given them permission to let go, are not as dramatic as I want to believe they are. In each case it was the right pastoral response, the organic next step, the natural thing to say. I feel no sense of power or control, only a sense of my priesthood as a mirror, which at its best reflects, without distortion of any kind, God's love for us.

I continue to hold on to a healthy respect for death. But I still ask the "what if" questions. What if it is all over when we take our last breath? What if we stop existing at that moment? The void, the emptiness, the nothingness all truly frighten me and leave me cold. I wonder if I am describing death or hell, or both.

To keep from becoming paralyzed by fear, I reassure myself that I cannot truly have faith unless I also have doubt. It is here, dealing with what happens after death, that my faith is strongest, because my doubting is most persistent.

Even as I tell myself that it is okay to be afraid and to wrestle with death, especially the death of a loved one, I wish that others would find solace in the struggle in their own lives. None of us will ever know for certain what lies on the other side. The resurrection of Jesus and our subsequent redemption can be accepted only in faith born of doubt, questioned by fear, and strengthened by love.

When death comes to someone close to us, it is good to have others to hold on to. Sometimes I, the priest, am that person. I will be there even if my own doubts remain.

Part Two

The Life That Shapes Lives

11

Dancing with God

Dancing is the best metaphor I can use to describe my relationship to God as God's priest to others.

NOT LONG AGO I attended a concert in downtown Chicago's Grant Park. The weather was perfect. It was a warm summer evening, a cool breeze blowing off Lake Michigan. As always, the view of the Chicago skyline was magnificent. The concert featured an interesting combination of selections by various German and Austrian composers. Included in the mix were many of the familiar and almost schmaltzy melodies of the waltzes of Johann Strauss.

Soon, some people began to dance. Some moved with an almost professional ease. A few young couples were content to simply move together, some more successfully than others. But the dancers I enjoyed the most were the older couples who had been dance partners for most of their lives. One would lead with great certainty while the other followed, completely comfortable. They would anticipate each other's moves effortlessly. Reacting consistently as one, the two depended on each other. I am sure that their dancing mirrored the exquisite give-and-take that was part of their successful, lifelong relationship.

I know of no better symbol to use to describe my priesthood. I have been dancing with God for three decades. And it seems that, increasingly, we are moving in unison across the dance floor that is life. It has taken me a while to learn that everything goes better when I let God do the leading. Unfortunately, the dance floor seems emptier than it should be—but appearances are deceptive. In reality, more and more men and women are dancing with God. Lots of ministry is happening. And that is good.

Over the years I have learned that God will lead me where God wants me to go and not necessarily where I expect to go. There have been periods when I have felt almost out of sync, painfully aware of every movement, gesture, and step. And then there have been times when my ministry has flowed smoothly, so certain that it appeared almost effortless.

That summer night in Grant Park I found myself watching one couple in particular. They were older, well into their late seventies, maybe even in their early eighties. But their moves were still strong and sure and graceful.

They anticipated many of the changes in the complex Viennese waltzes. They switched easily from one step to another, needing no words to communicate what they would do next. I expressed to a friend how sad I was becoming as I watched them. They were, after all, up there in age, and so much of their dancing was behind them now. How much longer would they have before failing health or something else sidelined them forever? My friend reassured me, commenting that dancing is something that takes place in the moment and that these moments would never be lost for either of them.

Having experienced the priesthood for thirty years, I know not to attempt to predict what will happen to it in the future. I trust that the Spirit will take us priests wherever we need to go. Some pundits predict a return to a more cultic form of priesthood, and others envision a wholly restructured form. I don't know who will be right. In the meantime, I have no choice but to continue to dance with God. I will not mourn the passing of time or the changes that have occurred or worry about what will be. I can only continue to live in the moment, trusting God.

Dancing is an apt metaphor not only for my relationship with God, but also for my ministry to others. We all need to remember that we best find God's loving presence in other people. Being a diocesan priest means that my life is caught up in the lives of many people. Not only do I dance with God, but I also dance with the other people in God's family, and they with me. The priesthood is something we experience together.

Three decades have given me a perspective that I did not have in the beginning. The children of the young men I taught in seminary are now enrolled in my parish school. This year I officiated at the marriage ceremony of the daughter of a woman whose wedding I performed a quarter of a century ago. Over the years I have baptized my nieces and nephews, and now I am doing the same for their children. And I am forced to remain quiet, as some of these children will not be baptized because of their parents' change in beliefs, which leaves me wondering if there was more I could have done. I have buried people I loved dearly—family, priests, friends, parishioners—and I've preached the Resurrection with all my heart, only to go home alone after the ceremony, filled with doubts.

Now more than ever, I am learning from the people with whom I share my ministry. As I get older, the natural instinct to become more cautious tempts me. But the faith-filled people of God challenge me to help them give more to one another and not to settle for less. I am comfortable in letting them minister not only to one another but also to me. I have learned that I am neither an invulnerable superman who can solve all problems nor a mysterious Shane who can ride into town, clean up the mess, and then ride off, a solitary hero, into the sunset. No, I am simply a partner in the dance.

Recently our parish book club read Graham Greene's *The Power and the Glory*. I remembered having read it in college seminary and being unimpressed by the whiskey priest running from his own demons. Now I admire him for the courage he did not even know he possessed and for his constant openness to minister to people no matter what the costs. Ultimately, it was their ministering to him that brought about the redemption that reflected God's power and glory.

I am realizing more and more every day that mine is not a solitary vocation. The God with whom I dance today may be a young father diagnosed with a serious illness or a woman who feels alienated from her husband or a congregation gathering to make sense out of a national tragedy or a group of children who are experiencing a sacrament called reconciliation for the first time. Or God may be a liturgy committee learning how to proclaim God's word or a fundraising committee taking on the responsibility of stewardship or a minister of care visiting a shut-in.

Who will it be tomorrow? I don't know. But for this moment the dance continues. And I remain caught up in it.

12

God Provides for Saints and Fools— and Priests

This young man's priesthood will bloom precisely at those moments when he takes his knocks and when the people demonstrate their love for him.

I F GOOD, HEALTHY PRIESTS are to stay that way, they need good, healthy priest friends. How's that for a banal statement? But it is true. The sad reality in my life now is that all of my closest friends, those with whom I could always share my hopes and dreams, those who would challenge me when I started taking myself too seriously and then prop me up when I started to sag, are gone. They are gone to death, to marriage, to the episcopacy. However, it has been said that God provides for saints and fools. I would have to add priests to that short list because we are located somewhere between the two.

God has a peculiar sense of humor in providing me with what I need. The priest with whom I can most comfortably share my hopes and fears, my frustrations and joys about priesthood is located halfway across the country. We stay in touch by phone, talking every month or so, and with an occasional visit. As calcified as my ministry sometimes becomes (I do fight to keep it fresh, but I don't always succeed), his is still new and vibrant, having just a year or so of priesthood under his collar. He has been able to create a wide support system for his ministry that includes a brother who was ordained more than a decade ago and who is a fine priest in his own right.

My friend, Bob, spent the last year before his ordination at the parish with me on weekends, helping with our ministries. A wise faculty member at his seminary realized that he had outgrown it and needed to spend less time there. He just had to get through it and get ordained. My job was to help him reach that point. His unabashed idealism brought to my mind classmates and friends from years ago. I worried that his idealism might turn into a kind of cynicism if people didn't respond to it. But they did. The parishioners overwhelmingly embraced him and in effect ordained him well before his own bishop did. I also worried that he might burn out, as I was not the most positive role model, being an overextended priest myself.

It became clear to me that my worries about Bob were more a result of my own desire to protect and maybe even modulate all of those wonderful pastoral qualities I saw in him. I did not want to admit that those qualities that made him so very vulnerable were what he needed to make him a good, strong priest. I gradually came to understand that protecting him would have been stopping him from being the kind of priest that God had called him to be. His priesthood would bloom precisely in those moments when he took his knocks and when the people demonstrated their love for him.

His final liturgy with us was an event. The church was overflowing, a sign of the parishioners' affection for him. In his homily, Bob mentioned how much my priesthood had affected him in such a short period of time. But I know it was so much more than my influence that led him to respond wholeheartedly to his call. At the end of his liturgy, I read a letter I had written to him, wanting not only him to hear it but also all those people present who had empowered him. I knew that once he was ordained, I would not be able to give him unbidden advice so boldly.

A few months later, I sat in a pew in the cathedral in his home diocese for his ordination. I am always uncomfortable at ordinations. By their very nature, they emphasize the separation of clergy and the people of God, a gap that constantly needs to be bridged, not expanded. So I sat there with many different emotions running through me.

I was thrilled that Bob would be able to experience the ways in which God's love would work through him and

leave its indelible mark on him. But I also knew the pain
his vision and style of priesthood would cause him—I
knew this because it was the very same priesthood I lived.
Being there with him, I was affirmed in a way I had not
been in years. But I was also conflicted, because the circumstances were causing me to look at my priesthood in
a way I had been able to avoid for years. Was this really
what I was called to do? Was this really what Bob was
called to become?

The church was very different when I was ordained.
The number of priests was increasing. The hope of Vatican
II was stirring the hearts of priests and laity. It was a time
when we priests felt that we were going to make a difference in the church and in the world. It was time to experiment in ways of ministering and of preaching the gospel:
"Behold, I Make All Things New." Who would have
dreamed that retrenchment and its abrupt fallout would
leave us stretched thin and so exhausted that creativity was
no longer possible—or acceptable, for that matter?

It came time in the ordination ceremony for all the
priests to come forward and, as a sign of solidarity,
impose our hands on those being ordained. After the
priests from Bob's diocese had come forward, I and a few
other priests from Chicago came up. I remembered my
own ordination thirty years before, when more than six
hundred priests placed their hands on my head and on
the heads of my more than thirty classmates. The number of priests who would place their hands on Bob and
on the twin brothers being ordained with him was much
smaller. As I walked down the aisle, I couldn't help but

wonder why anyone would want to do this with his life at this particular moment in the history of the church.

As I imposed my hands on Bob's head, I whispered, "This is from the people of St. Josaphat Parish, whose lives you profoundly touched, . . . and from me." Walking back to the pew, I looked out at all those patiently expectant and joyful faces in the pews, and I was suddenly reminded that we priests are all called to our ministry by the people of God. They are the ones who ordain us day after day, year after year, decade after decade. Why God chooses us will always remain a mystery. But answer the call we must. And then, with one another's support and with the love of God that is given to us by God's people, we must do the best we can. I walked back to my pew, finally at peace with myself and with Bob's choice.

13

A Candle in the Window

Too often, evil wins not because it is strong but because it is better prepared than the forces of good.

S A CHILD growing up in the fifties, I would sit in front of our old RCA television set and watch in black and white the pretty simple shows of those pretty simple days. Sitting next to me would be my Italian grandmother, who never really bothered to learn much English. But she was an avid fan of TV Westerns. They were easy to follow. The good guys always wore white, and the bad guys wore black hats. She would scream at the screen and swear at the villains in the dialect she brought with her across the ocean.

I have learned over time that evil is not so easy to spot. It is sophisticated and can hide itself behind an innocent-looking face or a compelling story. It can mesmerize and hypnotize. It is incredibly subtle and seldom direct. It surrounds itself with good intentions, logical arguments, and seductive phrases. But when it is unmasked, the sheer horror of it is something to behold.

Evil frightens me. Honestly, it scares me speechless. It is a power I never relish having to confront. But because I am a priest, there are times when I do not have a choice. At a neighborhood meeting a few years back, I was forced to look evil in the eyes. It was there in the form of a man dressed in a meticulously tailored suit. The meeting had been called so that community members could discuss the planned relocation of a transitional housing center for homeless women to the neighborhood. As the man came to the microphone and spoke in opposition to the relocation, I could see him simultaneously feeding and getting strength from the ignorance, hatred, and prejudice of many in the gathered crowd. How I wanted to eloquently throw down the gauntlet and destroy him with powerful, exact, prophetic words. But I was too shaken. I could only turn away in impotent disbelief.

Evil too often wins not because it is strong but because it is better prepared than the forces of good. It is more clearly focused. It is unafraid of what anyone will think about it. Evil is single-minded, pushing everything aside to reach its goal.

The relocation of the transitional housing center almost became a closed issue after that neighborhood meeting. Too many people appeared to be against it, and so it was rejected by the alderman. But the nun who was working to open the shelter was determined to convince him to reopen the issue. Because of my working relationship with the alderman, the nun asked me to accompany her on a visit to his office. At our meeting he was clearly distracted, patronizing her and ignoring me. We pushed. He held firm. We pushed harder. He finally agreed. But he gave us a dire prediction. He told us that in his opinion, we did not have the stomach for the battle that lay before us. That image of evil in a tailored suit flashed before me and I felt an icy shiver run through my body. I had a feeling that he might be right.

We gathered those who supported the shelter and began slowly, with planning sessions supervised by trained organizers. We held press conferences to showcase our growing strength and developing relationships. We visited neighbors and polled the community. Then somebody suggested that we pray. So an old-fashioned prayer vigil was organized. It would also be a media event, as we planned to travel in a procession from the church to the hoped-for location of the shelter—an empty convent a block away. A lit candle would be placed in its window and left there until the powers that be made the right decision to approve the relocation of the shelter. With so many clergy members from so many denominations actively supporting the shelter, I was surprised to be called upon to lead the concluding prayer of the vigil, which would be offered at the door of the convent.

What would I, the priest who had fled from the presence of evil, have to say? How would I pray over and confront that very evil? How could I, left speechless at previous meetings, come up with what needed to be said? My task was to adequately express the attitude and the intentions that had brought all these good-willed people together. I feared that whatever I came up with would be lame or, even worse, self-serving.

Just a few days before the vigil, I received a telephone call from the alderman. He was angry. Someone had distributed fliers questioning his ability to recommend a fair vote to the zoning commission because of certain alleged contributions that opponents of the shelter had made to his reelection campaign. He was talking to the wrong person, because I knew nothing about that level of politics. He insisted that I call "my people" off. I calmly told him that whoever they were, they weren't "my people." I pointed out that those fighting him were ordinary folk who saw a good thing in the shelter, people who did not have a political agenda, people who would not give up until they had a fair and just hearing. As our conversation ended, I found myself chuckling, and I couldn't help but remind him of his earlier prediction. I wondered out loud who it was now who didn't have the stomach for the battle.

So it was that I found myself on the doorstep of an old convent that had once housed women of faith who had heroically responded to God's call. God willing and if we did it right, this building would once again house women making a heroic response—to all that life had dealt them. I looked over the crowd and into their eyes and saw amazing goodness and sustaining hope. How could I be afraid? No evil, no matter how strong or vicious, prepared or willing, could penetrate the wall of grace around us.

As I began to utter the closing prayer, I seemed to step out of myself in order to listen to what I had prepared. As the candle, with its small, flickering flame, was placed in the window for all to see, words started to soar away from me. In a cadence unusual to my style or situation, people started to respond with vigorous amens and then to repeat the words that were coming from somewhere deep inside of me, somewhere unknown to me. When I ended, there was silence, only silence. Everyone was looking at that candle, and all of us were smiling victoriously.

We were smiling because we knew that we were going to win. And win we did. Today, Deborah's Place is more than a light in the window. It is a grace-filled reality that brings light to an entire community.

14

Empowered

*Like my father, who wanted me to be able to
take care of my own material needs, I want
the faithful to be able to take care of their
own and one another's spiritual needs.*

MY DAD CAME TO AMERICA in his teens with
few bankable skills, little education, and no
funds. He did not have to go through Ellis
Island because his older brother was already here and had
a job waiting for him. My dad labored in the coal mines of
Pennsylvania until he was nearly trapped and had his two
front teeth knocked out by a large chunk of anthracite. The
gold teeth that replaced them made him look more like
Don Corleone than a neighborhood grocer, which was the
job he held for most of his life. Between his two careers of

miner and food merchant was a brief stint in road construction in southern Illinois.

Because of his history my father firmly believed that his sons would not truly be men until they were capable of being independent and supporting themselves. He reminded me of this a few years before I was ordained, leaving me speechless and feeling that he did not appreciate my seminary studies. In actuality he was testing me to see if I really knew what I was doing and if I was truly committed to it. Until I had been a priest for a number of years, I didn't understand that Dad's concerns for me were much the same as my concerns for the people in my spiritual care.

Once my classmates and I were ordained and given our parochial assignments, a group of us came up with a homily theme for our first weekend Masses. We were going to invite the people to *allow us* to be their priests. It would be only when they let us minister to them and their families that we could actually be priests. In short, *they* would have to decide to ordain us. These homilies seemed to be very well received. I know that when I preached that message, I felt like a revolutionary, breaking down the barriers of too many years of harmful clericalism. But experience and time have given me an entirely different perspective of ministry and priesthood.

At every baptism I celebrate, I am now acutely aware of the prayer that proclaims that each of us is baptized *to share* in the priesthood of Jesus Christ. No longer is it enough to say to the people of God, "Here I am, your priest, and I am good. By your actions you should ordain me as your priest." It just isn't that simple.

Some of the profoundest moments in my priesthood have occurred when I have helped people realize that they have an opportunity and a responsibility to minister to one another. Like my father, who wanted me to be able to take care of my own material needs, I want the faithful to be able to take care of their own and one another's spiritual needs. It is not my job to do everything for them. Initially, the people of God who make up a particular faith community may have to empower me to be their priest, but it is only so that I may help them find within themselves the ministry that they are called upon to share with one another.

Good preaching is always helpful in bringing people into church. But eventually it is *their* stories that will need to be told. There are obvious times for this—mothers could share their stories on Mother's Day, fathers on Father's Day, veterans on Veterans Day, and married couples on Valentine's Day. Those whose sacramental marriages grace all of us should play substantial roles in the marriage preparation of engaged couples in the parish. Ministers of care should include those who have experienced what it means to feel helpless and alone while in a hospital. Those who have created truly Christian families should be the authors and presenters of the baptismal preparation program.

Let the finance committee share the good news and the bad with the community and challenge everyone's pattern of giving. Let the hospitality committee receive and welcome all newcomers. Let the community raise up gifted laypeople to become catechists and deacons and other leaders.

This is not just about letting people do bits and pieces of my ministry so that they will feel good and I will have additional free time. It is about people taking genuine ownership of their church and parish. Having learned this, I would now take a different approach in my first liturgy with a new community of faith. I would say to them that their acceptance of and openness to me would make my ministry obsolete—not create it—and would open the way for them to take the necessary steps to make their parish viable. We priests must constantly remember that there is no church without the people of God. We will then be liberated to center our ministry on the Eucharist.

While there continue to be insufficient numbers of ordained clergy available, more and more people are recognizing their role in this shared priesthood of Jesus Christ. To me, this is how the Spirit is working, and I am willing to let the Spirit carry this as far as necessary. There is no reason to be afraid of where all this will lead. In this respect, these may be the healthiest times in the modern history of the church. This mutuality of empowerment brings about an awesome synergy that may frighten some who see the church as unchanging and who want all the answers spoon-fed to them. But ultimately we will become a whole community celebrating together, rather than groups divided by titles, ranks, codes, and externals. There is power here, and grace and potential far beyond our comprehension. The church will make it. Now I know how Dad felt. It won't be the easiest of times. But there is reason to hope.

15

Learning Good Politics

A pastor has to be practical enough to engage in politics when it counts.

MY JOB AS A PASTOR has forced me to learn a lot of things I was never taught in seminary. We weren't offered business courses back then (and a parish *is* a business, in a sense), and we weren't taught how to engage in politics, which has come to make up a significant part of my ministry. There is parish politics, and there is community organizing, both of which occupy a lot of my time. In my thirty years as a pastor, I've had to educate myself in these areas—and it hasn't always been easy.

Community is about taking a disparate group of individuals and creating with them a united whole that operates from a common ground. For me, creating community has become a very spiritual process. As a priest I am coming into a community that has not selected me. I have been appointed to a post, and I am usually replacing someone who was well liked or, at the very least, respected. I have no history with these people. So I need to find out who the leaders are in the community—not only the movers and the shakers but also those who work quietly behind the scenes. And then I must take the time to meet with them individually. This also allows them the opportunity to check me out. Because they are so familiar with the community, they fill me in on the people and situations in the parish. This helps me determine whom I need to keep in my prayers, gives me starting points for conversations with parishioners on the church steps, and helps me break down cliques and bring people together. It is a time-consuming commitment, but the payoffs are invaluable. There is no short-cut to such payoffs.

Building relationships within one's parish just might be the most important thing a parish priest can do. For one thing, we cannot do everything on our own. I became acutely aware of this when I attended a ten-day training program at Fordham University in New York City. It was developed in the forties and fifties by the late Saul Alinsky and the Industrial Areas Foundation. It remains the premier community-organizing force in the United States today. Wherever you go you will not be far from a city or a region where ordinary citizens have been trained to listen and respond and act, often being Davids to the Goliaths that are big businesses, special-interest groups, and unresponsive government bureaucrats. Many of these community organizers come together initially through their churches, synagogues, and mosques. The program at Fordham brought together the most successful community organizers in the United States to share their experiences and help attendees develop the necessary skills and vision to foster healthy communities.

A simple session on time management forced me to look critically at my calendar, which was choked with meetings I felt I had to attend. More important, I examined my attitude. My actions were conveying to everyone that I saw myself as indispensable and that they did not have the skills to succeed without my being present to lead them. That paternalism is a dangerous thing, and many pastors get stuck in it.

At the training program I was also taught that we are all basically motivated by the same core interests— whether they are safer work environments, better schools, or more peaceful neighborhoods. And those interests can become the glue that holds together an otherwise diverse group of people. We can come together around certain pivotal issues that affect us all, and we can work together on them rather than constantly reminding one another of our differences.

To do all of this, we must build relationships, and that takes a great deal of time and patience. We do this primarily by meeting with one another; learning about one another's history, needs, and concerns; and then discovering the interests we hold in common. While this sounds easy to do, it isn't. It takes a great deal of discipline, active listening skills, and the ability to ask the right questions. Most of all, it takes time, lots of time. But done properly, it creates the strong foundation necessary to move us forward as a united group.

The bottom line is that the priesthood is a shared ministry between the priest and the people of God. I want to be the most effective priest I can be for the people I serve. I know some don't like the adjective *professional* put in front of *ministry* or *priesthood*. But I want to do my job in the best way I can. It's important to remember that being a priest is not about having power but about empowering others. Every baptism communicates to people that we all share directly in the priesthood of Jesus Christ. So my ministry should include a lot of letting go. It is liberating for all involved when the liturgy committee organizes a morning of reflection for all liturgical ministers. As the parish council grows in confidence and the social justice committee grows in vision and other groups crystallize their identities, I am amazed at the power that is released. As a pastor I'm in the unique position to orchestrate such community and create an environment where this can happen.

On the flip side of the coin that is my political life is my work with the larger community. I like politics so much because I was born and raised in Chicago, where local politics has always been colorful. The legendary Tip O'Neill once said with certainty that all politics is local.

A legendary Chicago alderman and pub owner once said, with confident arrogance, "This city ain't ready for reform yet." Both are right. Residents have learned how to play the system for all it's worth. And that is also necessary for those of us trying to do good ministry.

When I arrived at St. Josaphat Parish, I made sure that I introduced myself to the two aldermen at a housing meeting in the church hall. One was a well-connected, old-style ethnic ward boss who was based in the Polish neighborhood in the west end of the ward. The other was a young, brash, so-called independent whose constituency in the east end of the neighborhood reflected his affluent Jewish background.

I had been at St. Josaphat's only a couple of months when, on a Sunday morning in October, the entire Chicago marathon ran past the front doors of the church. The race blocked traffic and worshipers for hours. Worshipers, including a busload of our elderly parishioners from a local senior residence, were stuck in traffic and could not get to the church. Mass attendance was disastrously low. Afterward I learned that a number of churches in the area had experienced similar problems, as had DePaul University, which was conducting an open house. Each alderman had approved the route through his or her ward, and since the street in front of our church was in the jurisdiction of the young, inexperienced alderman, I decided to have a talk with him. He assured me that he would look into it and take care of it for the next year.

Ten months later, however, when the newspapers printed the route for the upcoming marathon, it was identical to the previous route, once again taking the race right past our front doors. I was angry. I brought up my concerns at a neighborhood meeting at which the alderman was present. He laughed it off, saying that it was too late to make changes to the route. So I invited him to imagine the Sunday morning of the race, the cameras on the lead runners nearing our church, when all of a sudden everything would grind to a halt, because our parishioners would be locked arm in arm across the street, protesting because they could not get into their house of worship on a Sunday morning. Standing together would be seniors with canes, mothers with infants, old and young alike. "You wouldn't," he challenged. "I would—I grew up in the 1960s," I responded. He invited me to a meeting at his office.

Eventually the route was tweaked so that no church or synagogue or major street leading to one was blocked. This was to everyone's satisfaction. Sometimes the local politicians have to be reminded of whom they are serving and who elected them.

Later this alderman and I teamed up and worked together on a number of projects. He solicited my support in keeping subsidized housing for those with special needs and for the elderly from being sold and turned into luxury condominiums. He learned that I could be a powerful and useful ally.

I have discovered that a good relationship with the local politicians can result in greater rewards than an occasional ticket to a Cubs or Bears game. Worked right and nurtured, it can save the parish money (when the alderman pays for new trees or sidewalks, additional lighting, or a needed stop sign) and can get us the necessary permits for parish festivals and many other important documents.

It is even good to know the folks in the local Streets and Sanitation office. I never know when I might need a special garbage pickup or a parking lot salted after an ice storm. These are important relationships to build. And sometimes they can be built over a few cases of beer on a hot summer day. Part of being a pastor is being practical, after all.

A philosophy teacher once convinced me that no one has power over us unless we give him or her that power. When I am dealing with the needs of people, be it housing needs or financial needs or health care or education or safety, it is extremely satisfying to know that I come with the power of the gospel and the cross. I don't use this power to bully anybody, but I do use it to make sure that people are heard and that their rights are respected. This most definitely is part of my work as a priest. It has to be. So my ministry remains very much local and intertwined with all that happens in the neighborhood and community. The local church needs to take an activist interest in the issues of the community. Developing relationships with the local politicians has always proved helpful.

My role is to train and help people to find their voice. Ultimately, they are empowered to take over, to provide the necessary leadership and earn the credentials to make a difference long after I am gone. And that is the way it should work.

16

Dancing with the Word

To effectively share the story of God's relationship to us, I need to be in touch with my own story and the stories of my listeners.

WHEN I STARTED OUT preaching, some thirty or so years ago, I was pretty bad at it. My homilies all came out as theology lectures—I was dumping on the people in the pews all the stuff that had been poured into me in seminary. Unfortunately, my delivery was no better. I began composing a sermon by writing it out word for word, as though it were a term paper, going through three or four drafts and squeezing the life out of it in the process. Once it was completed to my satisfaction, I would set about memorizing it—all of it, including the punctuation. From the podium I would "preach" by rote, reciting everything that was on the sheets in front of me without changing anything. It was all very stilted. For some reason, I was determined never to look down at my notes, no matter what. They were there "just in case." This pattern went on week after week for close to a year—a very long year.

Eventually I realized that the only way things would get better was if I moved away from the restriction of the podium. So I followed my usual procedures—including lots of theology in the sermon, writing everything out, memorizing it word for word, and putting a copy of it on the podium—but instead of standing in front of the podium I tentatively stepped away from it and recited the memorized homily from the center aisle. Leaving the copy of the sermon on the podium was irrational, I know, but it remained my lifeline: I could run back to it if ever I went completely blank, which was my greatest fear. That was never destined to happen. Knowing my notes were there offered me the security I needed.

Still I knew that I was not making much of an impact on the congregation. When I started my homily, I could see them reaching for the bulletin. Or they would just sit there with their eyes glazed over. Most damning of all, they would come up to me after the liturgy and say the worst words a homilist can hear: "Nice sermon, Father." You do not want to hear that, ever. One Mission Sunday, when a nervous nun in a veil and habit read her twenty-five-minute-long reflection while another nun stood mutely at her side to support her, a parishioner came up to me after Mass, grabbed my hand and shook it, and said, "Nice sermon, Father." I wondered aloud if he had noticed that I wasn't the one wearing the veil. It was becoming increasingly clear to me that I had to change my style of preaching, and soon. Besides, the research, writing, typing, and memorizing were not only eating up a lot of hours each week, but also were giving me a headache each weekend. I had to discover a better way.

My first step was to seek out the best preacher I knew and ask him for advice. He pointed out that if I insisted on writing each homily out, I would be tempted to save it and use it again. And in his mind, that was disastrous. Then he asked me how the Spirit could be a part of my sermon if all people heard was what I had memorized and not allowed to change or be taken where it might need to go. I knew he was right. Still, changing my approach was a slow process. But eventually I was able to integrate ideas into my prepared sermon as I preached. It took some time, but finally I was able to just leave some general notes on the podium. And after a while I admitted to myself that I was never going to go back to the podium to check my notes. So I came to preach with what I wanted to say in my head and in my heart, yet also prepared to be spontaneous enough to give the Spirit room to roam.

This new style had an immediate effect on the content of my sermons. It did not mix well with the theological jargon I relied on so much. In any case, I had started to run out of theological points. Fortunately I stumbled upon—or the Spirit kindly led me to—something called theology of story. At that time, authors such as Jack Shea and others were creating a new way of looking at what the story of our faith means. Its premise, simply stated, is that to effectively share the story of salvation, of God's love for us, that is found in Scripture and in our tradition, a preacher needs to get in touch with and be familiar with not only the word of God but also his own story of faith and the stories of the people with whom he shares his thoughts. I believe it was during that difficult period of growth that I first became a storyteller.

My homily eventually became a kind of spiritual dance, with my story touching the stories of the people to whom I preached. And together we explored and shared the mystery of *the* Story, found primarily in Scripture, but also found in human history. What a difference this new approach made. No more headaches. Now I was eager to make those connections that were building up inside of me.

Over my three decades of priesthood, I have given thousands of sermons, homilies, and reflections. I never grow tired of preaching. Who else has not only a captive audience on a weekly basis but also countless opportunities to reflect on the most pivotal moments in people's lives?

I continue to hone my skills. I know how to be dramatic and build to a climax. I know how to juxtapose pathos and humor to make the seriousness of what I am saying even more pronounced. I can use repetition and parallels to hammer home a point. I seem to know instinctively when to raise or lower my voice, speed up or slow down, and insert dramatic pauses. Timing is important. Used correctly, it can bring about gales of laughter and sobs of disbelief.

Most important, however, I have learned that a good homily comes from the heart. Often I am preaching something that I myself need to hear. Anything less than complete honesty will not only shortchange the listeners but also will destroy the power of the message. When the sermon is just not working, I give it a quick ending. It can't be fixed while it is being presented. All I can do is promise myself that I will do better next week. Even Sammy Sosa can't hit a home run every time he comes up to bat.

But when it all comes together—the opening story (which connects me with the stories in the pews), the message (during which I proclaim God's love for us), and the application (where I urge us to do something, now)— and all of this is combined with the power of the Spirit, it is exhilarating and humbling at the same time.

I am working on next Sunday's homily as I write this. I begin with a long period of silence. I pray that it will all come together. I've learned that the harder I try, the more I push the Spirit away. So the dance of the stories— mine and yours and the story of faith—is also a dance with the Spirit. If the people coming out of church next Sunday simply say to me, "Nice sermon, Father," I'll know I have failed. If they start enthusiastically sharing their stories and insights with me, then I'll know that we're dancing. And there is no better feeling.

17

God and Car Salesmen

*I encourage people to haggle with God. It
indicates a comfortable, familiar relationship.*

EVER SINCE **I** CAN REMEMBER, I have enjoyed
haggling over the prices of things. This is probably because it is in my blood. While visiting my
family's hometown of Alberobello, Italy, a few years ago
for the annual feast-day celebrations, I walked around
the holiday market listening to and observing the locals
and the merchants in their booths laugh, cry, scream, and
whisper until a mutually agreed upon price was reached
for everything from men's underwear to spark plugs.
When I was in Rome, the businesses that seemed empty
were the ones that displayed signs indicating fixed prices

on all items. But everywhere else tourists were eager to impress one another with their bargaining ability.

In Italy, the only way to really shop is to haggle. Unfortunately many tourists lack the finesse necessary to work out a bargain and a mutually agreed upon price. An item simply will not be sold if the proprietor has been insulted by an initial bid offered too quickly and with too much finality. Haggling in Italy takes not only the right words correctly modulated but also pauses placed at the appropriate places, perfectly executed sad looks, knowing sighs, and almost imperceptible gestures. It is an art, in short, that runs in the blood of most Italians.

My oldest brother was able to haggle for a living. He worked as a procurer for the Department of the Navy, haggling over contracts daily while never losing the respect of the contractors who did business with the Navy. Consequently he received all sorts of honors, awards, and medals upon his retirement. He once helped me purchase a car I didn't think I could afford. I watched and learned. He was like a hot knife slicing through butter; the poor salesman didn't have a chance. Before we left the dealership with keys in hand, the salesman gave my brother a free set of CorningWare dishes (even though I was the one who had purchased the car). That's how good he was.

I have to admit that unless I spend three hours with a car salesman, I have not, in my mind, done my job. It really makes no difference if I come out with a new car or not. While I don't wear my Roman collar to the show room—that would give me a distinctly unfair advantage—

if it seems that the fact that I am a priest will help me close the deal, especially if it has stalled, I'll find a way to casually mention it. I don't shy away from using my identity as clergy when that helps.

A soon-to-be-ordained intern working at the parish had heard my haggling stories and asked me to look at a car he was thinking of buying from a local dealer. In my estimation he had already worked out a very good price. But you know how it is. I had just come from a frustrating meeting with the cardinal. I was in one of those "stay away from me" moods, which must have been apparent, because the salesman broke out in a sweat when we appeared at the dealership. The intern introduced me as his pastor, which undoubtedly added some tension to the mix. The salesman's Italian name made me think that this was going to be a real challenge. But that wasn't the case at all. As we took the car for a drive, he told me excitedly that the tires were new. But I had already checked them as a bargaining point, and I knew they weren't. He had lied and thus had thrown down the gauntlet. When we got back to the lot, I told the intern—who obviously (too obviously) wanted the car—to just sit in it quietly; then I took the salesman aside and made my pitch. He countered with so little that I was able to threaten to walk away, throwing in a few expletives while doing so. He panicked and gave in, much to the surprise and the satisfaction of the intern. As we drove home in his new car, I felt a great sense of accomplishment that is hard to describe to the uninitiated.

I find that I frequently bargain with God in the same way. As a priest, I see it as part of my responsibility, one of my roles. In many cases, the priest is the link between a person and God. And all too often, that person will be hesitant to tell God not only what he is feeling but also what he really needs. So I try to tell this person that it is perfectly all right to bargain with God. It is an important part of the relationship that we have with God that makes haggling comfortable. We read about people doing it in the Old Testament, such as in Genesis 18, when Abraham drives a hard bargain with God. Throughout it all, Abraham is never anything less than totally respectful. Jesus and little Zaccheus carry on this tradition in the New Testament.

Such bargaining can sometimes be an indication of genuine affection. It happens quite often in families. In high school, I'd call home with six of my friends gathered around me and tell Mom that I was with twelve of my friends and that I wanted them to come to our house to play cards. Could she make pizza for us? I knew she would say no, complaining about the large number. So I would suggest ten. "No!" How about six? That she could handle. I think we both knew that six was my original number. She needed to set boundaries but also was pleased that I was bringing my friends over for pizza.

I believe that in the same way, bargaining with God indicates our affection. It requires a certain intimacy with God, which is lacking in many people's lives today, given our busyness and general distance from God. When we haggle with God we are relating with God, showing our faith in and familiarity with God. I tell people this, and that if God starts making tough demands on us, it is okay to ask God for something in return. I have a few caveats on this. The first is that haggling with God can be a lengthy process, as God does not deal in human realities like time and calendars. God works in God's own time. The second caution is that sometimes the prize we haggle over may bring us more demands than we'd expected. Finally, I tell people that God is a master haggler with an incredible sense of humor—and this sense of humor tends to show up when we least expect it.

It may be presumptuous of me to lead people in this direction. I do not intend to be disrespectful. This is what has worked for me in my relationship with God. It doesn't make sense to squander the simple human skills I have for negotiating on mere car salesmen. These haggling skills should be brought to the more sublime tasks of life as well. I'm at peace with applying my talents to all the parts of my life, especially to my priestly calling.

18

The Healing Touch

While the current headlines about priests make it a struggle, I need to remain confident that I can use the power of touch in my ministry.

I HAVE A LITTLE CONFESSION to make. Don't think me weird, but sometimes I stay awake well into the night and watch the religious programming that is broadcast on cable television. I am not at all intrigued by the sleek televangelists with their expensive suits and cheap wigs. Rather, I am drawn to another type entirely, those direct descendants of the old tent revival faith healers. I know that some of them continue to attract large crowds despite having been proven to be charlatans with radio receivers tucked behind their ears. And I know that others count on the communal emotionalism of the moment to capture people's imaginations. As I watch one of these healings, I am aware that there is something false about it. But regardless, something inside me wishes I could take away another person's pain or ailment—his or her devil—with a simple touch of the hand.

In my experience, it never happens that easily. When people come to me with their problems and their hurts, they usually come requesting prayers. I can give them that, but I have to make sure that I do not become overwhelmed by what is set before me. There's a Peter, Paul, and Mary song in which someone offers to take on another person's sorrows. Years ago, this was my highly romanticized notion of my ministry. But it isn't always possible to take on another's burdens. I have learned that often the best, and maybe the only, thing I can do is pray, no matter what the prognosis.

Still, there is something spiritually therapeutic about the human touch. Too many people go too long without the warmth and consolation of a connecting touch. Take the widowed seniors gathered for a meeting. Perhaps the only person who has physically touched them all week is a hairdresser or doctor. A hug from me, my hand placed in theirs, a kiss on the cheek, my palm on their shoulder, my help as they walk down the stairs—all of these are simple ways of communicating my care and concern for them.

While the current headlines about priests make it a struggle, I need to remain confident that I can use the power of touch in my ministry. I cannot be like one of those Chinese doctors of old who used an ivory figurine of a woman to help an embarrassed female patient point to where her ailment was. My touch can reach right to the heart and to the spirit and thus become a salve for a person in pain.

That touch, combined with the almost primordial, soothing power of oil, is at the heart of the sacrament of anointing of the sick. One Saturday evening at a parish communal service, it was my profound privilege to anoint more than a hundred faithful who had gathered, each with his or her personal ailments and concerns. As I touched their arthritic hands and looked them in the eyes or I anointed their foreheads with the blessed oil, I encountered a faith that was truly healing. I found that I was being healed as I moved from individual to individual. I was barely able to keep my emotions in check. I found myself watching as one woman gently took a little of the oil I had placed on her hands and on her forehead. She gently dabbed her eyes with it. A while back she had told me that she was worried about her deteriorating eyesight. That simple act of faith on her part brought me to tears. I truly wished that she would tell me at that moment that her sight was fully restored. But that is a sign of my lack of faith.

Healing is not about instantaneous physical change. Most of the folks I anointed at that communal service have died as the years have passed. Yet I know that what happened on that evening brought about genuine healing in many of their lives.

I believe that much of that healing had to do with the physical connections we made. As I, the conduit, transmitted God's love and grace to them, they were sharing the power of their faith with me. Those were sacramental moments that made a difference in all our lives.

In some ways what I do is even more miraculous than what appears on TV and at revivals. During those moments when I offer to others physical touch with my hands, the healing they bring moves beyond the physical symptoms to those wounds of heart and mind that are even more crippling. And I feel God's loving presence as I touch others with the very grace that heals so profoundly and personally.

19

Port-a-Potty Questions

*Who else but the parish priest could decide
how much a Port-a-Potty holds?*

PARISH FUNDRAISING EVENTS serve two important purposes, in my mind. The first, of
course, is financial. While every pastor wishes
for a financial situation in which weekly worshipers give
regular donations that cover the parish's expenses (and
with leftover money going into a contingency fund), it's
rarely like that. We have to rely on fundraising events to
help us survive.

On the other side of the coin is the community-building
aspect of a fundraiser. There is something so unifying
about working with the members of your parish to raise
money for needed repairs and expenses. While it would

be nice to focus our energies on building, strengthening, and educating the community, the truth of the matter is that we have to spend a lot of time raising money. Two of the best byproducts of this are the bonding among parishioners and the bonding between a congregation and its pastor.

Our parish has been fortunate. We started out very small but have rebuilt and have grown at a steady pace. We have been able to deal with financial problems as they arise and before they get out of control by rallying the community around various needs and honestly telling them what fundraising must be done. Early in my pastorate I learned that my role in these activities would need to be that of the cheerleader who energizes everyone, supports them, and smoothes over the feathers that inevitably get ruffled.

Each year on one of the weekends that fall between Father's Day and Independence Day, the parish throws an outdoor event called, most unoriginally, "Summerfest." I wanted to call it "The World's Smallest Block Party" to playfully tweak Old St. Pat's Parish and play off its nationally known and very successful "World's Largest Block Party." But the original committee voted that down.

Over the years, Summerfest has grown to a comfortable size: we close one short street block for the stage, the food vendors, and, of course, the requisite beer truck. Behind the church in our beautiful park we set up tables where people can sit. The parking lot houses the silent-auction tent and the Kidsfest. Even the gangway between the church and the rectory is transformed into an old-world bistro.

We did just fine with all of this for a number of years. Parishioners generously volunteered for setup and cleanup. More than 250 volunteer slots would be filled through the weekend. Beyond the weather, which was out of our control, there were seldom any problems. Because we were in a residential area, we shut the festival down at 10:00 P.M. It was typically a relaxing, enjoyable time for everyone involved.

One year, however, we signed up a band that had become a favorite of some of the Chicago Bulls players and so had gathered a large following. (We had contracted them at a very reasonable *pre*fame price.) The crowd that showed up at Summerfest on the night the band played was far bigger than expected.

The beer truck was doing big business, which meant lots of profit for us. But where there is beer, there must be bathrooms, and the only bathrooms we had were the two that are located in the basement of our school. We were not ready for what happened that night. At one point the president of our parish council came running out of the school, shouting that people were urinating on the stage, in the corners of the auditorium, and in garbage containers in the lower hall. We shut down the beer truck and narrowly averted what could have been a disaster. Fortunately no fights erupted. With the beer gone and the music over the crowd went looking for other places to party.

We knew that we would have to come up with some viable solutions for the next year's festival, the first one being to sign up a less-popular band. We decided that we would lock our buildings to all outsiders and rent a row of Port-a-Potties that we would discretely locate on the grassy area between the sidewalk and street, away from the crowds. Being new at this, we had no way of knowing how many Port-a-Potties we would need. Of course, a monumental decision such as this would rest squarely on the shoulders of the pastor. My initial instinct was to gather all the pertinent information.

I decided to consult the architect in charge of festival logistics, a very patient parishioner. But just as I was about to ask her, with a straight face, how much a Port-a-Potty holds, I realized how ridiculous a question it was. Even if I could obtain that information, I would have no idea what to do with it. I'd know how much it would hold, but I wouldn't be able to determine how much people would likely put *into* it. My postgraduate studies had not taught me how to make such calculations. So I just stopped midquestion. I'm glad I did.

What I almost asked became the joke of the fest's wrap-up party. As it turned out, the dozen Port-a-Potties we had rented were more than enough. But we did make a note that, in the future, we should tell the company that serviced them every morning to flush them out well before the outdoor Sunday liturgy. Their timing that first year could not have been worse.

It is silly issues like Port-a-Potties that highlight for me what community is all about. Some people might think these things trivial, but even the little things are important. When good people, busy people, give up their entire weekend to volunteer for an event, and when they start working on it days, weeks, even months in advance, I am reminded that the Catholic Church consists of its people first and its pastors second. These parishioners who volunteer their time must really love the parish and feel committed to the community that they are a part of. And while their dedication reminds me that I don't run the show, it also confirms that I am doing my job. I have preached the gospel, and the people of God have responded.

They have so many other responsibilities; they don't have to be here. Because of this, I feel that I can never thank them enough. Words won't suffice, so I make sure I am present and visible whenever they are working. How can I think of taking a break if they are working for what is ultimately my responsibility? They have taken ownership and don't see what they are doing as a burden. In fact, they enjoy themselves, and as a result, so do I. A bond of friendship and respect grows even as we sweat through our Summerfest sun visors. So we laugh together and smile a lot during the event. And their pastor becomes an accessible human being in the process. Not a bad byproduct of it all.

This is what community is all about. It doesn't always have to be the serious stuff that brings us together. Cana, after all, is a pretty good example. Jesus' first public miracle was turning water into wine so the wedding feast wouldn't be spoiled. I bet the apostles couldn't wait to follow him after that.

20

Sitting It Out

Leading people in prayer takes an energy that just cannot be faked or drawn from a tank that is empty.

O N THE SECOND FRIDAY of each month, our parish offers an hour of Taizé prayer. This form of prayer was established by an interfaith community in Taizé, France, that for decades has been attracting young people. The format of the prayer is wonderfully simple: it combines hypnotically repetitive music and responses, the glow of candlelight, peaceful silence, and beautiful icons. I am never sure where my prayer will go during the hour, but I usually find myself taken someplace sublime and surprising. I am not alone in my feelings—this style of prayer has become very popular in many places.

There's another reason I enjoy Taizé prayer so much: instead of standing apart from everyone, I get to sit with them. It's a great honor to lead people in prayer, but it is also hard work. Sometimes, especially when I am tired, my energy goes toward leading the prayer and not the prayer itself. It is so easy to get distracted, to start worrying about the homily or whatever comes next. *Is there a Gloria intone? Why aren't the gifts being brought up?* It's a real luxury to be able to just sit back and pray and not have to be "on," to allow my thoughts and prayers to privately take me wherever they want me to go. Taizé prayer requires no leader, no celebrant, so I can pray without being responsible for saying anything or doing anything or remembering anything publicly. I am able to simply pray alongside everyone else. That's a real gift to me.

So much of my prayer is public prayer. Sometimes it lifts me up and I know that I am blessed—and I hope the congregation is as well. Sometimes the best I can do is just be there and go through the motions. Too often I find that I am distracted; but, ironically, there are many times when I feel one way and later learn that those praying with me have felt something entirely different. Call it God's grace. I am just grateful that God chooses to make good moments happen even when I am floundering.

This holds true for liturgies, celebrations of the sacraments, and even incidental moments when people simply ask me for a prayer or blessing. I am finding that it is especially hard for me to be a real leader of prayer on those days when I have two or three Masses, three weddings, and a couple of baptisms. Leading people in prayer takes energy that just cannot be faked or drawn from a tank that is empty.

For me, one of the great joys of being on vacation is getting to be just another member of a congregation and not having to lead others in prayer. Even if the liturgy is less than what it could be I am able to relax and pray, getting into myself while also enjoying the company of the people in the pews around me.

Being on the congregation side of the altar gives me a different perspective on what it means to be in church. I experience some services that are dynamic and others that aren't, but I learn from all of them—if I'm paying attention. And I hope that each time I sit in the pew I go back to my place behind the altar a better priest. For one thing, I learn much about what makes a liturgy effective for the congregation.

I once attended Mass in a church in Lake Tahoe that had a window behind the altar offering an exquisite view of the mountains and the lake. The service itself was not so captivating. The visiting priest was unable to figure out the mysteries of the microphone. The volunteer organist was clearly unprepared, and no one stepped forward to proclaim the first reading. As the homily wandered for what seemed longer than the Jews wandered in the desert, I looked around. Young parishioners and old, families and couples, solitary figures—all were paying better attention than I was. I came away from that service

with a sense of who the faithful are, how patient and forgiving they are, and how without them my own imper-
fect priesthood would mean nothing at all. I promised
at that moment in silent prayer to always try to be as
prepared and focused as I could be when I celebrated
with them.

Across the country, in northern Maine, I attended Mass
in a church where the old celebrant looked like a fisher-
man who had just stepped out of a Winslow Homer paint-
ing, his face as craggy as the coastline itself. His accent was
so thick that I had to concentrate to understand every
word. His inflections kept going up when they should
have come down. But his warmth and sincerity burned
through. I was disappointed when he announced that he
wasn't going to preach. An old missionary friend of his had
come to deliver an annual funds appeal.

Out of the sacristy came a short, stout contemporary
of the pastor, carrying, of all things, a clarinet. He told us
almost shyly that at the end of a day of work in the missions, when he was missing home and all its comforts, he
would take his clarinet down to the ocean and play
"Stranger on the Shore," and it would comfort him. He
told us that this song would be his sermon and appeal to
us that day. We all listened, spellbound. When he finished, he gave us an awkward bow and walked off the
altar. I gave him all my vacation spending money. What
a message.

As Mass ended and the recessional hymn began, the
old pastor scooped up a young child from his mother's
arms and carried him on his shoulders; together they

resembled the image on the old holy cards of St. Christopher and the Christ child. Not a soul left the church until the final note of that hymn was sung. I attributed that miracle to the quality of the liturgy. (But I did notice that the gated parking lot was locked from when Mass began until the pastor had processed out of the church.)

Once the congregation was outside, so many people gathered around the pastor, now with the child in his arms and his missionary friend at his side, that rather than try to greet them I simply waved and smiled, silently proud to share my faith and profession with these two men.

I have since carried a child or two out of church on my shoulders. I have never been blessed with a musical mission appeal. And our parking lot doesn't lock. But when I am tired or distracted I think of that simple liturgy in Maine and that patient, faithful congregation in Lake Tahoe, and I am grateful and joyful that I can give the people of God my best. And then I try to kick it up a notch for their sakes, and for mine.

21

Celebrating the Family

As a celibate priest, I grow old, in many ways, alone. It is one of those challenges that define me.

NOT TOO LONG AGO, my family gathered together. The occasion was simple: my oldest brother, who lives in Virginia, had come home for a rare visit. It gave us an excuse to break what would turn out to be a lot of bread together. Over bowls of pasta and meatballs we caught up and reminisced. There were four generations present; we ranged in age from six to ninety-three.

We talked about a lot of things and laughed about even more. I found out that my brother who is only three years older than me dyes his gray eyebrows brown. My other brother had just gotten a new pair of bifocals. Our conversations seemed to revolve around our changing appearances, and it struck me that this was because many of us around the table were growing older.

Someone else must have realized this as well, because an old video appeared that had been made close to two decades earlier. It was a recording of a family celebration combining Easter and Mom's seventy-fifth birthday. It was shot with what was then a newfangled contraption called a camcorder, and we were all obviously self-conscious about being recorded.

Time was magically turned back. There we were, my brothers and I, without any gray hair—and the hair we had was significantly longer. We were pounds lighter. One of my sisters-in-law realized that on the video she was only a year or so older than her daughter, who was now sitting next to her watching it. My father appeared on the video like a ghost—the recording had been made less than two years before his death—and thus returned to the family briefly like a lost memory. Mom was the one who had changed the least, looking as incredible for her age back then as she did this night. On the tape she remarked that sometimes she felt as if she were close to a hundred years old. At the time that we were watching the video, she was very near that age. Watching the video, my somewhat confused six-year-old grandnephew, Joey, grabbed my feet and held them.

La famiglia. Family is everything to us. And if that is an Italian stereotype, so be it—without apology. The media may want to turn us into loud, dumb Mafioso types. But in our Italian family reside dignity and love.

I drove back to the rectory that night alone. After all these years as a celibate, that is the usual routine. I remembered how I used to drive Mom and Dad to their place, but that was a long time ago. Driving alone gave me an opportunity to do some melancholy thinking. In my life, there would be only one nuclear family, the one I was born into. I would not be able to create my own family with a loving wife as my brothers had done. I had watched my brothers' families expand as their children started their own families. As close as I felt to all of them, I knew that when my mother died, my feelings would be a little different from theirs—they would at least have their own families to go home to. This realization hit home a few days later, when Mom suffered a small stroke. She recovered, but the experience left me frightened of what I knew would inevitably happen.

And happen it did, just a few months after our gathering. It was quick—another stroke, a fall, a broken pelvis, a brief attempt at rehabilitation. Conscious and alert to the end, my mother's last words to me were "I love you all." Nothing could have prepared me for the loss. It is still too soon for me to even begin to put my feelings into words. That will happen later, someday.

As a man without a family of my own, I must face life a lot of the time on my own. But even as I acknowledge the challenge, I recognize that there are blessings too. My ministry has afforded me entry into so many lives and families over the years, and these connections have helped me through many moments of aloneness and loneliness. We who are ministers can be ministered to greatly by God's people, if only we let them into our lives and hearts.

A warm and caring priest once shared an important insight with me. He said that of the priests he knew, the healthiest—and therefore the most effective—were supported by families that remained touchstones of reality for them as well as sources of love, affection, and intimacy. He believed that the emotional and spiritual support of family gave priests balance and confidence in their ministries. Since his much-too-early death before the age of fifty, this priest's own family has continued his ministry through scholarship funds for the seminary and parish in which his priesthood blossomed.

My family remains an oasis of calm for me when my life begins to spin out of control, when I begin to feel sorry for myself, when I wonder if I am capable of being loved or am loved. Once the kid brother who was always on the outside, never old enough to join in with his siblings, and told he was a pain, I have finally become a peer, and that is so important to me. Now my family members even dutifully show up for my book signings. I feel that I am finally able to give back some of what they have given me. Family dynamics don't change too much. I'll always be the youngest, spoiled kid. While I hate it, I know that it's okay. We all just play the hand we're dealt.

My sisters-in-law, I figure, have never fully understood me or my life. I am similar to my brothers, their husbands, yet different. Perhaps they find it odd that I have such a mysterious lifestyle but at the same time am so much like my brothers. My brothers and I have the same history, the same value system, and the same supports. Yet I turned out very different from them. I'm sure my brothers' spouses are perplexed by this difference between them and me and have questions that will go unanswered because they don't want to ask them: *What is his sexual identity? Couldn't he handle the responsibilities of a family? What does he really value?* But as I get older, I feel less mysterious to my family and more accepted.

My parents' deaths have affected my ministry more than I ever imagined. Dad distanced himself from his sons after his daughter's death, and perhaps I mirrored that remoteness with my choice of a celibate priesthood, which by nature is distancing. At the same time, Mom's nurturing nature, which was a constant in the more than nine decades of her life, also affected me. When she told me that of all her children I was the most like her, I cried. She could have paid me no greater compliment.

My family continues to mold and shape me and thus be an integral part of my ministry and priesthood—more than they realize, I'm sure. Without them, I could not do what I do and be what I am. And now that applies to a whole new generation—my nieces and nephews and their children. To them, I am Uncle Dominic the priest. One of my nieces, at age ten, told her friends that I had to become a priest because I was so ugly. There is truth in children's insights. But ugly as I am, my family accepts me—and not only that, but they also love me, and that brings me peace and confidence as I look toward growing old, alone but not really.

22

Me and My Body

Rectory life is not really conducive to healthy living.

THE WAR BETWEEN ME AND MY BODY has raged on for years. I put on weight. I take it off. I don't care how I look. I become very self-conscious. I jog, only to succeed in compressing two discs in my back. I attempt to swim but only sink. It seems that when I was younger I merely fought a skirmish here and there, battling my body for vanity's sake. I remember learning that a full beard could hide a lot of chins. But when that facial hair turned gray I had to make another choice. I shaved it off. As the years have passed I have come to realize that the real issues are health and quality of life, not charisma and good looks.

So now the battle goes on even more intensely than when I was younger.

If I had been a priest forty years ago, it would have been harder for me to fight this battle. When I was an adolescent, I began to notice that some priests had a unique smell, especially those who appeared to be holy and somewhat otherworldly. There was a musty smell about them that reminded me of the smell of the water in the holy water font at church, which was never changed. Their combed-back hair appeared gray not from age but from infrequent washings. And their clothes, mostly cassocks or black suits, were shiny and faded at the same time and usually revealed that the wearers had a dandruff problem. These priests coughed a lot, the same cough my brothers hacked after a cigarette or two, but the priests' coughing was more frequent, almost chronic. They spoke softly, using as little breath as possible.

There were two other kinds of priests when I was growing up. There was the occasional jock priest who was always in a sweatshirt except on Sundays and who even on Sundays smelled like Bengay. And there were the monsignor wannabes, whose presence was announced by the scent of Old Spice cologne mixed with Brylcreem. They were always dressed in cuff-linked shirts and perfectly pressed black suits. Some were older, but a surprising number were quite young. And they never walked anywhere their black Buicks could take them.

Most priests clearly did not take care of their bodies. Their days off would almost always consist of drinks and a steak dinner and then more drinks with other priests. During the rest of the week the rectory cook would try to live up to her self-ordained calling to fatten up the fathers by cooking everything—breakfast, lunch, and dinner—in butter.

Back then, most priests' only exercise was an occasional round of golf. Heart attacks seldom changed lifestyles. There was little in rectory living that was conducive to good health.

Times have changed. Now many priests, including me, work out at gyms or health clubs. Some of us even use a trainer. And while I still carry much more weight than I should, I try to stay in touch with my body, because I know that my health is in my own hands. (A distinct disadvantage of the single life—no other person looking out for one's physical welfare.) I know that when I reach a certain weight, I don't look good and that the excess weight isn't good for me.

I've noticed that there are numerous bonuses to exercising regularly. The discipline it takes has had a positive influence on my prayer life. When I exercise I turn inward. I become very quiet. I get into the "zone," as it is called. I do my time on the elliptical machine or treadmill with my eyes closed. When people remark about this, I just tell them I am praying or meditating. Often, problems I bring into the gym with me find a solution before I leave. Usually I simply let the exercise take me wherever I need to go and do not interfere.

I've found that I cannot exercise in a gym or health club close to the rectory. Parishioners won't let me out of the locker room. It seems that guys like to talk to their priests in the safety of that environment, which means that my designated two hours for working out pass and I've never made it to a machine—in fact, never left the locker room or even changed into my shorts. So I work out across the city in a small, nondescript gym above a plumbing supply store.

It is good for me. My neurotic need to be in control of everything, including my body, has led to a fear of doctors, which I am constantly working to overcome. Exercise helps that fear to subside. I accept my body with all its limitations.

Now arthritis is setting in, in my knees and other joints. Exercise is keeping me flexible. I still fear the unknown things going on inside this body. But I acknowledge the reality that my body is part of who I am as well as a vessel that can lead me to God. Living with my body can be hard work, what with celibacy, aches and pains, and having to work out. When I want to give up, I think about St. Paul, who used a lot of athletic metaphors and talked about the "race" of faith. I'm never going to win any races. But I don't want to finish the one I'm in just yet. I don't need to understand the mystery of my body; I just need to accept it. And then comes the peace that carries over into my ministry as part of another body—the Body of Christ.

23

Pauses

Like everyone else, I have to create pauses in
a too-busy life. How else can I keep going—
in a healthy way—in this life to which I
am called?

SOMEONE ONCE TRIED TO PAY the legendary
pianist Arthur Rubinstein a compliment by asking
him how he made all the notes he played sound
so beautiful. He said with a smile that the notes were not
as important as the pauses between them. There's a
lesson in that statement that I'm trying to live out.

Most all of us, unless illness or some other uncontrol-
lable force limits us, are living busy lives. It may be a
Day-Timer or a Palm Pilot that controls our days (and
nights as well). Or it may be the ongoing needs of a three

year old and a nine month old in the same household. Our responsibilities are such that when someone, innocently or patronizingly, suggests that we slow down, we give him or her a wistful smile, thinking to ourselves that we are not choosing to be as busy as we are, at least not consciously. In any case, we are not in the position to make a full lifestyle change, not just yet.

I know that my life is busy. But in reality I am no busier than many of the people I encounter on a daily basis. I know that a good deal of my time is self-scheduled, whereas others' time is affected not only by their own schedules but also by the needs of their families. I know that I'll never have to worry about finding a babysitter or help a teenager with a difficult math problem.

But I do have those three-wedding Saturdays when an occasional funeral slips in or somebody wants me to bless his or her new car after Mass. And then there are those seemingly "small" requests, like that of the parishioners who want me to hear their confessions before they leave to visit their daughter-in-law. Some weeks I have to prepare a special graduation homily, a funeral homily, one basic homily to be used at three weddings, and a regular Sunday Mass homily. That is a lot of preparation.

Parishioners by and large recognize how busy their priest is. They tell him, "Father, you are too busy. You have to slow down." Unfortunately, these good-willed folks are the same ones who insist that we stop by their meeting or activity or prayer service or whatever, confident that we won't let them down. And they refer their family members from other parishes to us when they need help, because we are nicer than their own priests. They know we won't mind helping. And of course, even though we do mind, we are flattered.

Some priests are skilled and self-possessed enough to be able to take a day off—often a full twenty-four hours—every week. I am not able to do it, for whatever personal limitations, but I know that I should. It is one of the areas in my life that I am still working on and struggling with.

But I do enjoy the time I am able to set aside for myself. Once I get away I am quite good at leaving everything behind. I have no beeper. My cell phone number is guarded more carefully than a cardinal's expense account. I don't feel the need to keep checking in at the parish to see how things are going. So that is one good sign.

In my life, pauses don't happen naturally; I have to create them. Often after celebrating a funeral and paying my respects, and as the undertaker finishes up business with the grieving family, I'll step away from the chapel or graveside just to enjoy the beauty of nature around me in the cemetery—the trees, the grass, the flowers. These few moments refresh me before I have to drive back into the city.

In the trunk of my car I keep a kite, one that folds up neatly into a small pouch. When I am returning from a hospital visit or a talk or a meeting on a windy spring or fall day, I sometimes decide to just pull off the road, park the car, and take the kite out. Watching it soar in the sky gives me a sense of personal freedom, as if it is me up there swooping and diving and climbing. I can be lost in it for hours.

While waiting for people to arrive at a meeting, I will pull out a notepad and start writing. It's amazing how many of those random thoughts and feelings that otherwise might have been lost can be captured and saved to use in a homily or somewhere in my writing.

I love to walk. At about the two-mile mark, the stuff of work seems to disappear like fog in the morning sun. My mind is freed up for me to pray or reflect on Scripture or think about family and friends. Sometimes I will stop just to study a gnarled tree. I am often surprised where my thoughts go at such times.

I have a friend who used to take a minimum of five to eight books on vacation with him. His goal was to have them all read by the time he came home. When I travel, I do not want to be burdened by any responsibilities, even if they are self-imposed. I won't take guided tours that force me to be at certain places at specific times lest I be left behind. Vacation time should not turn into work. When I take time off, I try to make as few decisions as possible. Someone else can pick out the restaurant for dinner. I must be either great to travel with or very frustrating. I don't put a lot of demands on my vacation partners. But I also refuse to make many decisions.

It is in all of these pauses, long and short, that I am able to step away and put into perspective not only what I do with my life but also why I do it. When I am relaxed and my focus is readjusted, my enjoyment of my priest-hood intensifies. Those pauses are integral and important parts of my priesthood. They are my times of prayer.

I have learned, as Richard Carlson observes in *Don't Sweat the Small Stuff at Work*, that after I die there will still be work left unfinished in my in box. These days I am working hard at working less so that I can pause more and enjoy more.

24

Pets

I advocate a pet for every priest; such a responsibility reminds us of all the things we don't have to worry about.

L ET ME BEGIN BY SAYING that I love animals. The parish's annual blessing of pets on the Feast of St. Francis of Assisi in October is a highlight of the year for me. It gathers a large crowd of people and a veritable Noah's ark of pets. The service in the Book of Blessings is appropriate, and our singing the Prayer of St. Francis accompanied by the sounds of the animals is touching. My own cat brings me great enjoyment. And, although auctioning off two puppies one year at a parish fundraiser was so controversial that some people refused to attend, the Jack Russell terrier, straight from the breeder, with all his shots and a year's supply of food, brought one of the highest bids of the evening, $1,600.

Many priests—including me—live like well-off bachelors. A lot of our daily needs are taken care of by others. It is easy to become spoiled by this and to take for granted all that others do for us. I think that priests would be better off if they were responsible for a pet, any pet at all. For one thing, pets give that unconditional love and affection that we are always preaching about. For another, pets remind priests of all the things we do not have to worry about. You cannot ignore the responsibilities of having a pet—they require time and energy and concern.

I have learned this firsthand. Many years ago, when I was still teaching, members of the graduating class decided to give me a gift. It was a black kitten with a small tuft of white fur at its throat. The students had searched for a cat that looked like a priest in a Roman collar and had finally found one at the city shelter. As I held him in my hand for the first time, he began to cry, sounding just like a priest friend of mine named Jerry who is now a bishop. I remarked that he sounded like a little Jerry, and that is how he got his name. Little Jerry the cat and I shared our lives and our living space for more than fourteen years until he died on the eve of the parish summer festival.

Concerned parishioners drove me to the city animal shelter just two weeks later to pick out a new cat. There, on a rainy day, (thus the name Stormy), a kitten found me, and for the last five years she has been living in my home—or perhaps it's more accurate to say that I've been living in *hers*.

Each pet is different. We need to know what we can handle. I love dogs. I am especially fond of retrievers and labs. But my ministry is in the city. My rectory has no yard at all. My private rooms would not provide enough space for such a large dog. Nor would I be around all the times that a dog would need to be walked. If this pet idea is going to work, it won't happen if the secretary does the walking and the janitor does the brushing. In fact no priest's pet should become a burden of any kind on the staff of the parish; otherwise, it defeats the very purpose of having a pet and it only adds to the problems and concerns in a priest's life. So there are rules that include: No puppies on the pastor's lap during dinner. No cats given free reign of the entire rectory. No fish being fed by the DRE every day. All of it has to be the priest's responsibility.

So Stormy, as well as providing companionship and being there for me to talk to after a long and busy day, also demands that I stop thinking about myself and change her litter box, feed her, freshen the water in her bowl, and clip her growing nails. In response to these and other favors such as my taking time to play with her, I receive wonderful returns.

For instance, she sits on my desk when I am writing. When she gets bored and decides that I have been working long enough, she puts her paw on my writing pad, forcing me to stop. I have no choice but to put down my pen, scratch her ears, and give her a little attention. It is amazing how this helps me focus on something besides myself, and so inspires my work.

My cats have sparked many homilies, icebreakers at gatherings of new parishioners, and much more. I know that having a pet, be it a puppy, a kitten, a bird, a ferret, or a fish, could go a long way toward humanizing us priests when we become too full of ourselves.

I could write a lot more about this, but Stormy is making me stop. She senses that I have made my point.

25

Meditating on Notre-Dame

I am a parish priest. I do not want to be a museum curator.

I HAVE NOT TRAVELED enough in my life. So when the opportunity arose to spend a week in Paris with a priest friend whose French-Canadian heritage (i.e., his ability to speak French) would help us get around much easier, I was eager to go. An overbooked seminary was a surprise blessing, as we were able to find rooms in a small, two-star hotel on rue de St. Jacques in the Latin Quarter. This meant we were only minutes away from Notre-Dame Cathedral. I wanted it to be the first official stop of my trip. Like the rest of Paris, it was all that I had expected and a total surprise at the same time.

As I made my way to the cathedral, I dodged beggars and tourists and probably some pickpockets dressed as tourists. The view from the Seine was stunning. My eyes traveled from the massive doors upward, noting features that had become familiar to me from the countless photos I had seen throughout my life. But seeing it stand there majestically in front of me took my breath away.

When I walked inside the cathedral's cool darkness, mysteries from the centuries surrounded me instantly. Where to look? Where to pause? Chicago has its fair share of cathedrals and stained-glass windows, but the colors of Notre-Dame's windows were at once vivid and deep and subtle, unlike any others I had seen. Each of the statues along the side altars of the nave was a work of art, each capturing a different moment or sense of faith from a different time in history. Catholics are always works in progress, never finished. Even the starkly modern Nativity scene, set in sand for the holidays and in stunning contrast to the surrounding classical artwork, was exquisite in composition. Behind the altar were paintings and carvings that told stories from Scripture and the lives of the saints.

One side altar had been glassed in, turned into an office of sorts where penitents could share in the sacrament of reconciliation. The local priest sat reading a book. The cathedral was teeming with people, but no one stopped to take advantage of God's forgiving graces in the sacraments, myself included.

Books, postcards, and slides were being sold at the souvenir stand. A few weary tourists sat on benches and wicker chairs to rest tired feet. It seemed that few people were praying. The din that echoed up to the ceiling came not from pilgrims lifting their voices in prayer but from sightseers pointing out treasures to one another. I left as I came in, one of the sightseers, although I had taken time for prayer.

One evening as it was growing dark, I had the opportunity to return to Notre-Dame by myself. My friend had gone in search of an antique print of the streets of Paris. I went in search of the sacred. The floodlights that shone on the cathedral cast an almost subterranean glow on the rainy street, making Paris at night look even more mystical. Once inside the cathedral, I surprised myself. Instead of walking around to look at all the treasures I had missed the first time, I found a much-used chair off in a corner in which to sit and pray.

I noticed a man deep in prayer, his shaved head tattooed with markings that would help a radiologist locate the cancer treatment. I knew where his prayers were taking him. An elderly woman was finishing her rosary, her loaf of dinner bread sticking out from the basket at her feet. I guessed that she was praying to her deceased husband. And so it went. I joined my prayers with the prayers of a number of people that evening, and I forgot the sea of tourists and sightseers walking all around me. They disappeared.

I remembered the statistics I had read about France's churches; reportedly, only 4 percent or so of the Catholic population in France attends worship services. Considering the amazing art both inside and outside the country's churches, I found it incredible that so few people actually worshiped in them. How could they have lost the mystery of God's presence, a mystery so brilliantly conveyed in the masterpieces all around them? Worse, how could churches as magnificent as these—built and maintained by people of faith over centuries as a reflection of their love of God—become museums more than living houses of worship?

I thought of my own church in Chicago, St. Josaphat, where I have been pastor for fifteen years. We had just completed a more than two-million-dollar partial restoration of the building, coinciding with the hundredth anniversary of the laying of the cornerstone. A hundred years for a church in Paris is nothing, but in Chicago it represents a long time. Our beautiful old church is admired by all who come to visit it. Twelve years ago it almost closed due to a lack of worshipers. But a gentrifying neighborhood and lots of hard work and evangelization have brought in new, young families.

So in Notre-Dame I said a prayer of thanksgiving. I am, after all, a parish priest. I do not want to become a museum curator. The beauty of Notre-Dame is timeless. But the beauty of any church filled with worshipers—who want to be there to share their joys and their concerns with a community of faith—now, that's eternal.

26

Kodak Moments

Having presided over thousands of weddings and baptisms and hundreds of confirmations, first communions, and graduations, I now appear in photo albums everywhere.

IN A WEDDING ALBUM probably gathering dust on some shelf, there is a portrait of me unlike any you will see of a priest in a wedding album. My head is tilted rakishly to one side, and I am flashing the brightest of smiles. A bouquet of flowers is resting against my cheek. It is as though I were hugging them. It isn't your typical picture of a priest at a wedding, but there is an explanation for it.

The events leading up to the snapping of that unique portrait were bizarre in their own right. We had run through the typical forty-minute wedding rehearsal, so I felt free to leave the church. But the couple's wedding coordinator, who was clearly being paid by the hour, decided not only to rehearse everything again, but also to change everything we had rehearsed.

At the ceremony the next day, I could see almost immediately that things would not go according to the way we had rehearsed them. The wedding planner had clearly had her own plans in mind. The wedding party started down the aisle couple by couple. But they were attempting to travel the ninety-foot distance doing the stutter step together. The girls had it down pat. The guys were out of step and stumbling awkwardly. Worse yet, it was taking each couple five minutes to reach the front of the church.

At a predetermined spot in the aisle, the groomsman stepped away from the bridesmaid, who took her bouquet and held it next to her tilted head so the photographer could snap a picture. Then the groomsman rejoined her and they resumed their stumbling journey to the front of the church.

Initially the congregation just watched in disbelief. But by the third couple, laughter could be heard above the organ and the trumpet. The whole thing became more ludicrous as the procession wore on.

I tried to ignore the fiasco, so I began the ceremony without any reference to the procession. It took great self-control. Usually, my pastoral instinct is to do nothing to embarrass the bride or groom. But that changed as I moved to the podium to read the Gospel. I had noticed the photographer running up the aisle to get a photo of each of the Scripture readers. I figured she would do the same with me. I had also noticed a beautiful bouquet of flowers that the bride was supposed to carry to Mary's altar later in the ceremony. It was well within my reach when I arrived at the podium. The moment the photographer ran up to snap my picture before I began the Gospel, I grabbed the flowers, tilted my head coquettishly to the side, brought the flowers up to my face, and smiled from ear to ear, just as the bridesmaids had done earlier. The flash went off and so did the congregation, laughing for a full five minutes. Even the bride and groom joined in—everyone except the wedding coordinator. I get a laugh imagining this photograph, strange as it must have come out, now in their album along with all the prerequisite shots. I hope an explanation is given when family and friends ask about it.

Often when I am invited to a parishioner's house, I see my picture on a shelf or bookcase or piano. It is a little disconcerting. While none of the pictures are quite as bizarre as that wedding portrait, there are plenty of me posing with a bride and groom or witnessing their vows. There are also shots of me baptizing babies, pouring the water on them or immersing them, as I now do. In some of the pictures I am posing with parents and godparents or I am holding the infant up to present him or her to the congregation. There are also first Holy Communion photos. But because I forbid photography during the ceremony, they are mostly shots taken on the steps of the church after the ceremony. The same goes for confirmations. But I usually have to share space in those pictures with the bishop, who has me outdressed with his miter and crosier.

These photos, taken at different times and places, reveal how my appearance has changed over time. For one thing, my weight fluctuates. My hair has grayed and thinned. In some pictures I'm wearing contact lenses and in others bifocals. My beard is now gone, revealing more chins than I care to believe are there. One constant is my smile. I clearly enjoy these sacramental moments, these special encounters with God, whose love I am charged with communicating. I look at a picture and wonder what I emphasized in my homily that day. Did I feel like I hit a home run, or was I distracted or out of energy from a long weekend of sacraments? Did I make them laugh? Did I find myself crying? Was I going through the motions, or was God also touching me as I performed the ritual and prayed the prayers?

I don't ever want to think about the number of wedding videos I'm in. But even if they can show every action and record every word, they can never get inside of me and show what I was feeling and praying that day. My various hairstyles and facial expressions might invite comments as people view my mug on mantelpieces and pianos over the years. But all those moments of projecting God's love just cannot be captured.

The numbers of ceremonies I have performed are overwhelming to me. My current stay at St. Josaphat includes close to a thousand weddings, more than two thousand baptisms, and hundreds of first communions and confirmations, not to mention graduations and other ceremonies. This means that my face stares out from a lot of frames in a lot of homes and family albums. I know that I am not the reason these pictures are displayed. I just happen to be in them with the important family members. Sometimes folks send me copies of these pictures, and I'll look through the pile of them now and again. These important milestones in people's lives ultimately blend together for me, and names begin to fade, as do dates.

Still these photos are colorful reminders of how I become part of people's most graced, sacramental moments. Although these ceremonies may be routine for me, they are special and important moments in time for the people involved. And so I can never allow myself to take what I do for granted. I must always give my best.

Part Three

The Grace
That Appears

27

God's Playful Presence

Some days, just being a priest places me on the defensive. Thank God for the occasional friendly poker game.

IT WAS NOT a nice phone call. It was the second one she had made to me. In the first she identified herself as a former parishioner who had worshiped in our church years ago. She was calling as a mother of a potential bride. She seemed to believe that her former membership gave her the right to demand that I marry her daughter in our church, no questions asked, on the date of her choosing. I told her that I would have to speak with her daughter, that it is best for me to deal with the brides and not the mothers.

Two months passed before the bride called me. Because she had waited so long, two weddings had been scheduled for the day she wanted. There was a third time slot available, but I was not prepared to take on a third wedding. I offered her the slot, but I told her that she would either have to find another priest to celebrate the ceremony or have a deacon perform it. The young woman said she would think it over and get back to me with her decision.

Instead, Mom called again. And she was really angry. How dare I not marry her daughter? How dare I tell her to find another priest to perform the ceremony? She was going to call the chancery and report me. I told her that if she stayed on the line for a moment I would give her the number and save her the call to information. This stunned her into momentary silence, and I jumped in to explain the situation. I pointed out that even though her daughter was not a parishioner—but was, in fact, someone whom I had never met—I had offered her the third time slot. But my full schedule would prevent me from celebrating her daughter's marriage.

The mother chose not to hear my explanation. When she snidely asked if I was too busy because I was being "indicted" like so many other priests, I was tempted to hang up on her. Instead I told her that her insults were not improving her daughter's chances of being married here, but I would not give her the satisfaction of making me hang up. This stopped her again. So I explained that as the only priest assigned to the parish, I simply could not do any more than I was doing.

This time she called me a liar, saying that she distinctly remembered four or five other priests working at the parish when she was a parishioner and demanding that I admit that this was the case. I was amazed by my composure. I was determined not to hang up on her. I simply asked her how many years ago that was, and before she could respond I asked her if she was aware that fewer numbers of priests had been ordained during the last few decades. I told her that many parish priests married only registered parishioners and that I had been trying to do her daughter a favor. But I would make no apologies for putting limits on my schedule.

I don't know if I calmed her down or confused her. I told her that her daughter should have called me eight months earlier to get the date she wanted. With that, the dam burst. It seemed that her daughter didn't really want to get married in the church; Mom was the one who so desperately wanted it. She lamented how much the world had changed. After my conversation with her, it was easy for me to agree with her on that. I invited her to have her daughter give me a call whenever she was ready. I assured her that we would find another priest to marry her if it had to be that date or we would find a slot on a different Saturday when I could do it. The conversation was over. She hung up, never apologizing.

I sat there not knowing if I should laugh or cry or pray. Part of me was very angry and part of me was sad. Worse than that, part of me was irrationally feeling a little guilty for not agreeing to perform the ceremony, even though it would be my third wedding for that day. I have always found it difficult to deny anyone the sacraments, regardless of the reason. Why did I try to defend myself to her? In retrospect, it might have been better if I had just hung up. I was feeling very alone. Who understands us priests?

At that moment, the phone, still in my hand, rang again. I did not want to answer it. I did not want to talk to another mother or daughter. In fact, I did not want to talk to anybody at all. But there I was, saying, "Good afternoon. This is St. Josaphat Church." Mercifully, the familiar voice on the other end was that of a parishioner who does a lot of volunteer work for the parish and whom I've gotten to know quite well. He was inviting me to join him and some of the other men from the parish for cards on Friday, immediately after—you guessed it— my last wedding rehearsal. God's playful presence comes to me in so many terrific ways.

That Friday we gathered and laughed and played cards until midnight. I knew I'd be tired the next day, when I was scheduled to celebrate two weddings and two other Masses. But playing cards that night brought me a real sense of peace, because I was with parishioners who accepted me as I was; I was able to let down my guard. It was well worth every nickel of the ten dollars I lost. I still felt lucky. I am learning that in my priesthood, I am never alone, no matter how lonely I sometimes feel.

Oh, and—you guessed it—the daughter never called back.

28

The Laughter
That Remains

Lifelong friends are irreplaceable, and the loss is especially hard when it involves those with whom you've shared a vocation.

JIM AND I REALLY got to know each other when we were sophomores together in the high school seminary. Initially our friendship was based on Jim's ability to drive us around. Since my three older brothers were of driving age, there was little chance I would ever be able to use the family car. So I didn't even get my license until college. Jim's dad had bought his sons a 1955 Pontiac that was built like a tank (he always said he wanted a lot of metal around his sons). That car, loaded with six or so seminarians, made it through snowdrifts and below-zero weather to somehow get us all home safely, even if it meant Jim kneeling in the snow and praying for the car to start. That was the extent of our mechanical know-how. Those years of driving home in Jim's car led to what would become a lifelong friendship.

I met Jack two years after I met Jim. We were assigned to the same dormitory in our first year at the college seminary. The two of us were quickly dubbed "the instigators." We succeeded in getting everyone else in trouble and were smart enough to step back to watch the fun without getting caught ourselves. Jack's "Who, me?" look would crack me up every time and his Irish blarney would inevitably get us out of any predicament. What I remember most about those years in the seminary is not the prayers or the classes but the pure, life-sustaining laughter that seemed to follow us wherever we went.

The three of us were ordained in 1973. After ordination we parted ways, heading off to our first assignments. It was only a few years later that Jack and Jim and I found ourselves back together. This time we were on the other side of the desks, as teachers in the high school seminary. My memories of those years are full of the same sidesplitting, eye-watering laughter that seemed to occur whenever we were together—much to the dismay of some on the faculty, who felt that we were not being serious enough about anything and everything.

One weekend the three of us decided to get away. Our stated goal was to rewrite the junior-class retreat. At the time, Jack was part owner of a summer home north of

Chicago. It was a cool autumn evening when we arrived. The frost in the air was, unknown to us, bringing inside all sorts of creatures that normally lived outdoors. Before long we began to hear scratching sounds in the walls and scampering sounds in the attic. We made a trip to the local hardware store—any excuse not to start our work— and purchased traps that would handle what we were told would either be squirrels (which we could deal with) or rats (which were another story altogether). We were told to bait some of the traps with cheese and some with peanut butter and to place them in the attic first. If the creatures were squirrels, they'd be caught by their paws; if they were rats, they'd be caught by their snouts.

We decided to draw straws to see who would do what task. Having drawn the short straw, I was the one charged with putting the traps in the attic. With a broom handle, Jim would prop open the attic door in the kitchen ceiling. And Jack would balance a short ladder on the table, which I would use to crawl into the attic. I had my doubts about our battle plan.

Nevertheless I donned a ski mask, gloves, a baseball cap, and a heavy winter coat for protection. I wasn't very mobile, but I felt safe. With a baited trap in each hand and a flashlight between my teeth, I carefully climbed atop the table, then up the ladder that Jack was holding.

Jim slowly opened the attic door with the broom handle. Tentatively I stuck my head through the opening, the flashlight still in my mouth, and surveyed the dusty floor of the attic. When the light reflected the eyes of some feral creature, I screamed, dropping the flashlight on Jack's head. He instinctively reached for it, letting go momentarily of the ladder. I yelled for Jim to give me the broom handle. I was determined to reach in and beat the creature to death. But Jim kept refusing to give it to me. I found out why the instant I grabbed it out of his hands. The door it was propping open came slamming down on my head. The ladder, already unsteady, shifted and caused me to fall backward onto Jack, who in turn fell onto Jim. The three of us fell off the table. The broom handle, followed by the ladder, landed on top of us, and we started to laugh so loudly that we could barely hear the sound of one of the traps, which I had also dropped, latching onto Jack's middle finger.

All that laughing made us too weak to try again. So we just packed up everything and spent the night at a Holiday Inn. The next day the exterminators came and removed, of all things, a family of raccoons that probably had come down through the chimney.

Honestly, I am not completely sure that this is exactly what happened that day at Jack's cottage. But it is the version that Jack delighted in telling, beginning with his description of me in the ski mask and ending with his finger extended in a splint for two weeks. Jack was a born storyteller.

Both Jack and Jim, two goodhearted and talented priests, are now dead. One died from AIDS and the other from cancer. Both would have been great storytellers in retirement. Death comes much too unexpectedly to people who are so full of life. Both of them could preach a homily you would never forget. Both were outspoken in their own way but unfailingly pastoral. Their funerals came much too early in their lives. I miss sharing ministry with them. Quite often I think about them as I am celebrating the Eucharist. And I slow down a little. And my voice grows a little softer.

I no longer ask the question "Why?" In fact, I don't ask anything at all anymore. What I do now is listen. And it always seems to come from somewhere—maybe from the choir loft or the sacristy or the confessional—but I hear the sound of their laughter, and once again they are making me smile. In that solitary moment, I feel good about the priesthood that we shared for so many years and that is still ours today.

But living without them remains hard. Lifelong friends are irreplaceable. Once they are gone, they are gone. New friendships may develop, but they don't have the same history and richness born of a lifetime of shared experiences.

29

A Voice Coming Through

When I preached the funeral homily for a fellow priest and close friend, mystery touched me in a way it never had before and hasn't since.

I DID NOT KNOW that someone in the congregation had taped the homily I gave at Jim's funeral until a few years after his death. The quality of the tape was poor. It was scratchy and had an echo that gave it an almost dreamlike quality. I cannot even remember who gave it to me. In fact, I listened to it only one time, and then, for reasons still inexplicable to me, I threw it away.

I think that I was afraid of it on some level, or maybe it was meant to be heard only once. I don't know for sure.

A few months before he died, Jim asked me to preach at his funeral. Although we were good friends, I was surprised and touched, and not a little uptight about being given the responsibility.

In the weeks before he died, he became very specific about what he wanted me to include in the homily and what he definitely did not want me to bring up. This was during the early days of AIDS, and Jim feared that his death from AIDS-related complications would gather the Chicago media and turn his funeral into a circus. Jim was afraid that people would remember only the disease that killed him and not all that he believed in and the ministry that had filled his eighteen years of priesthood.

So, by his orders, I was to mention the disease, but I was not to linger on it or make it the focus of my homily. Because his mother was still alive, he did not want me to bring up the cause of his illness. I didn't, and as a result I received an angry letter from members of Dignity (a Catholic gay activist group) saying that I was part of a "conspiracy of silence." But in fact I was only following Jim's wishes, which I will continue to do now, as I relate this story.

On the day of Jim's death, I holed up in a little room in his rectory where he had died. I thought and I prayed and I wrote. Around me was swirling the issue of whether Cardinal Bernardin would attend the funeral. His advisers, wanting to protect him from controversy, kept giving contradictory reasons why he could not fit the wake or funeral of one of his priests into his schedule. I really think he wanted to be there. But the advisers won out. I stayed out of it. I just worked on the homily. At three o'clock in the morning after the wake and before the funeral, I finally stopped. I had in front of me a couple of homilies, a eulogy, a manifesto, and a biography. Clearly I had written too much. I didn't know how I would be able to cut it all back, but somehow I managed to trim it down.

There was some tension in the church before the funeral. Jim wanted no one serving at the altar except his closest friend, who would be the main celebrant, and me as the homilist. This caused a few of the auxiliary bishops to get bent out of shape. As the church filled to overflowing, a moving testament to a priest who had touched many lives, all I could do was watch the hands of the clock in the sacristy move inexorably toward 10:00 A.M.

Finally the time came. Usually I like to preach and I consider it a great privilege. But as I looked at the coffin, then at Jim's mom, and then at the congregation that had empowered his priesthood, I decided I did not want to be standing up there. No words could possibly do justice to or make any sense out of what had happened and what people were feeling.

Two years later, as I listened to the tape of the homily for that one and only time, I realized that I had gotten my wish. I *wasn't* there. The preaching style was not mine at all: the cadences, the word choices, the constant use of parallels, the pauses, even the inflections—it just didn't seem like me talking. Listening to the tape, I discovered that I had subconsciously mirrored Jim's very distinctive preaching style in my reflections on the Scripture and on him. It became clear to me why I couldn't later reconstruct what I had said. Is it too melodramatic or presumptuous to believe that Jim spoke through me?

After hearing that tape, I understood why I didn't know how to respond in the church hall after the funeral when friends came up to me and commented on the homily. A lawyer who belonged to a prayer group that Jim and I had been a part of embraced me and said simply, "Well, if you ever hoped to become a bishop, it's gone now with that homily." I didn't know what he meant by that, but it made me feel good deep inside. And when the chancellor of the archdiocese called me and asked for a copy of the homily, I had to tell him that I had not written it out and could not reconstruct it. It existed only during the moments when I was preaching it and in whatever bits and pieces people remembered.

That homily was one of those invaluable moments when a priest realizes that he is no more than an instrument that God chooses to play, a tool that God uses to create something. This truth was the most evident during that mysterious time; I haven't experienced grace in quite the same way since. It was both unexpected and humbling. I know that there is no way I could have planned it to happen that way. But something tells me that Jim did.

30

Listening to the Oldies

A long drive and the right radio stations
opened the way for hours of good prayer.

TECHNOLOGY IS SUPPOSED to make life easier for all of us. But I'm not sure it's helping me. I'm often overburdened by all the demands that are placed on me and that I place on myself. There are all the voice mails to answer, on my office phone as well as on the private phone in my room. There would be voice mails on my cell phone too if I didn't refuse to give out that number. I save that phone for emergency calls or calls that I choose to make from my car. And now there are also the e-mail messages that I must reply to, personal e-mails as well as those for the parish, all of them meeting in some magical way on my computer.

Nobody ever seems to be in when I try to return the calls and messages. So I am forced to leave a voice mail, thus starting the process all over again.

It isn't just the quantity of messages that overwhelms me, but also the seeming disregard people have for my time. It is the 7 A.M. phone call from a woman wanting to know if a particular Sunday is available for a baptism. It is the noon visit by the young woman who decides to stop by on her lunch break—without an appointment—and meet me to decide, I guess, if the color of my hair will match her wedding flowers. Does she ever for a moment think that I might be eating lunch?

I used to sit in church before morning Mass and take that time for prayer and reflection on the coming day. I would enjoy the sun shining through the stained-glass windows. But people kept coming to me and interrupting me with their questions and observations. So now I hide in the dark sacristy, where I am still found and interrupted, but not as often.

Admittedly, much of this is my own fault. I can find very little middle ground between being accessible as a good priest should be and turning into a self-absorbed bachelor who doesn't want his life to be interrupted at all. I slide between the two extremes depending on my mood and fatigue level.

Every few years I come to the point when I realize that I've had enough for a while and I need to get away from all the demands. When this happens, I pick a destination that is at least a full day's drive away. Flying won't do because I need to physically experience the distance between me and everyone else. Only driving seems to accomplish that for me. Being alone in a car with lots of miles to cover and no way of being interrupted is just the right solution.

I used to listen to books on tape or CDs to keep my mind occupied. But recently I took an eighteen-hour road trip to the East Coast, from Illinois to New Hampshire. And as the miles passed, I did something different: I searched the radio for the oldies stations. They were easy to find. Every market seems to have one. There are the oldies of the forties and fifties, on what are called "beautiful music" stations. Then there are the stations that play the jamming rock 'n' roll of the sixties, with all its great rhythms and harmonies. Last is the classic rock of the late sixties and early seventies, which radio stations treat almost as sacred music from a sacred era.

As each song came on, I would think about the first person it brought to my mind. I would try to recall one memory of that person, and before the song ended I would say a prayer for him or her. For instance, when the Rolling Stones's "Ruby Tuesday" began, I thought of Ruby, my beloved "other mother," and all the wonderful advice she would give me. I said a prayer of thanks for all the years we were able to share our faith before her death. Then I started talking to her, asking her for advice once again. I did this with many people over many miles. Some of the folks who came to mind were dead; others were still a very important part of my life. Sometimes the person who came to mind would be a complete surprise to me. Most of them had affected my priesthood in some way. If a person came up more than once during the drive, I had no trouble coming up with another memory, and I figured that he or she was in need of another prayer, which I was happy to give.

Sometimes I prayed in thanksgiving for the memory or in gratitude for a time of real friendship. I often found myself chuckling, and occasionally I got teary-eyed. With some people, I had to turn off the radio in order to reflect more deeply on a set of memories. It was like being on retreat. What an easy way of connecting with those who had touched my life. What an enjoyable way to recapture graced moments that could have been left under the cover of forgotten or nearly forgotten memories.

It is hard to describe all the different feelings I experienced during that trip. All I can do is suggest that you try it yourself. If oldies music doesn't work, try whatever does—classical, jazz, dusties.

After five or so uninterrupted hours of contemplation, I pulled off the New York Turnpike and got out of the car. I was struck by how connected I felt to others as I stood there alone and still hours from my destination. And that connectedness brought me real peace. My priesthood has woven my life into the fabric of many others' lives in a profound way. I must never lose sight of that in all the responsibilities of my day-to-day life. I need to keep it all in perspective. And listening to the music and celebrating those memories helped me do just that.

God does this to me all the time—brings me the sacred through the ordinary and close-at-hand. I didn't discover any new theology about prayer, only a new doorway to the genuine experience.

31

Corking the Whine

*If I would just pay attention, I could see God
answering prayers all the time.*

I FIND THAT WHEN I GET BUSY, I get tired, like most folks. But when I get tired I tend to look ahead in my schedule, and if it is full, I get even more tired and overwhelmed in anticipation of everything that is going to happen. It becomes a vicious circle. My defenses begin to crumble. I start feeling sorry for myself. And, worse than that, I begin to vocalize my self-pity. In short, it is no fun being around me. I start to whine and I expect everyone around me to put up with it.

Not too long ago on a particular Friday, I was starting to feel really down. The day was quickly jamming up in more ways than I had anticipated. All of a sudden I found myself rushing out to do an anointing of someone I did not know. I glanced over at my desk. It looked as if a bomb had exploded on it. As despair and the sense of being out of control began to wrap around me, I said a quick prayer, asking God to just get me through the day.

Then I drove off. Usually driving calms me down. The car can be a good place for me to focus and to pray. But on this day as I drove to the hospital all I could think about was all I had to do. Everything was interrupting everything else. The anointing went extremely well. The family was appreciative of this and other times I had been there for them, even though I could not remember them or those times.

When I returned to my desk, an employee of the parish was waiting for me. His presence usually means bad news. Either a large check is needed for supplies or something major is wrong with the plumbing or a boiler didn't pass inspection. I could afford his services only part-time, so our parish split his hours with a neighboring parish. On this day he just wanted to thank me for being a good boss. He said that he appreciated working for me and in such a stress-free environment. It was a nice, unexpected compliment.

Later, as I completed my second wedding rehearsal of the night, I noticed a parishioner at the side door of the church watching me intently. His oldest daughter had just left for college. He was probably filled with mixed emotions. We decided to go out for a beer after I completed the third and final rehearsal of the night. I moved things along briskly.

We went to a local pub for food and beers and—more important—conversation. It was good to spend time with him. As I walked home, I thanked God for the friendships that had formed for me in this parish.

Nearing the church, I noticed a police van parked out front. Two officers, both of whom recognized me, were interviewing a street person about an assault that had happened earlier that day downtown. The man's clothes matched the description given by numerous witnesses of the clothes worn by the attacker. He looked at me, scared and confused. I remembered that he was at our door getting something to eat at the time they said the assault occurred, so the cops released him on my word. He stumbled off looking mightily relieved. As the cops and I stood talking, a call came in that the guilty suspect had just been captured miles away. I walked into the rectory feeling surprisingly good, thinking about how much I liked being a city priest.

And that was when I finally realized that my prayer had been constantly answered throughout the day. Many good things had happened, evidence that God had more than helped me "get through the day." This realization gave me a little more faith that God would partner with me to make good things happen in all the busy days to come.

32

Little Gloria and the Glory of God

Every time I hear the name Gloria *or hear the "Gloria" sung, I am reminded of a grieving family's faith—a faith that touched me, the priest who was there to minister to them.*

PEOPLE'S LIVES ARE FILLED with pivotal and life-altering moments. As one who ministers to others, I am often called to share in these personal experiences of change. And in a mysterious way, I too am changed.

I experienced this mystery intensely with one family in particular. I was invited into their lives by the eleven-year-old daughter, who called the rectory one day. As we talked, I was impressed by how polite and mature she sounded. She clearly had rehearsed what she needed to say to me in order to get the message right. Her parents were not comfortable speaking English, so she had become the spokesperson for the family. And thus it was left to this child to tell me that her new baby sister was born not only prematurely but also with many other problems. The prognosis was not good. Would I be able to come to the hospital to baptize her? I knew that I shouldn't ask this child more questions than necessary, so I told her to tell her parents that I would be there within ten minutes.

Traffic and a full parking lot at the hospital, however, made me forty-five minutes late. When I entered the hospital, I was sent directly to the neonatal unit. I was stressed and concerned. I did not want to be too late. I immediately recognized the parents. The father attempted a smile, and the mother looked terribly weary. They appeared older than most couples with newborns. Fortunately their English was much better than my Spanish. And their young daughter was there to bridge our gaps.

With sadness in their voices, they told me that their newly born daughter was not expected to live another day. Aside from being born prematurely, she had seriously underdeveloped organs, a damaged heart, and Down syndrome–related complications. There was no chance of survival. But the family was at peace because I had arrived to baptize her.

The compassionate and competent nurses prepped us. We scrubbed down, put on our gowns and masks and gloves. I was given a small, sealed bottle of distilled water to use to lessen the threat of infection caused by bacteria. We were told to leave the baby's little knit cap on her head as long as possible to keep her from losing precious body heat. Mother would be the one to hold her baby. I was given only three minutes, the maximum amount of time she could be out of the incubator.

And so we began. The mother, with the first gentle smile I had seen on her face since I had arrived, indicated that she had dreamed of this moment. It was the first time she had been allowed to hold her child. I asked the parents what name they had given their daughter. "Gloria," the father replied without hesitation. He then explained that she was an angel poised to return to God's glory. He was smiling and crying as he shared these words with us. A moment later, the little child of God, now christened Gloria, was back in the incubator, struggling for each breath. Her sister looked at me hopefully as I was leaving. "Now Gloria really is going to be an angel, isn't she, Father?" I assured her that she already was. That night Gloria died. There was no wake, no Mass of the Angels. For the family, life goes on. People learn to cope even as they carry their sorrow with them.

A few months later, the parish's seventh and eighth graders participated in confirmation, the sacrament that makes sacred the transition from childhood to young adulthood. It was a warm, uplifting liturgy. I was proud to be the pastor of this group of young people proclaiming their faith before the congregation. The bishop did a good job of taking time with each of the candidates, often asking about his or her chosen confirmation name. When the bishop asked one of the seventh-grade girls what her confirmation name was, she stepped forward and replied proudly, "Gloria." The bishop selects different students to stop and talk to at more length—every fourth or fifth one. I wanted him to hear Gloria's story, so I stopped him and prompted him to talk with her further. She told the story of her baby sister, who had lived for only a day. "My sister is the glory of God," she remarked earnestly, "and a true saint." The bishop told her that she could not have picked a better name. As he confirmed her with the sacred oils I stood there with tears in my eyes.

At the deathbed of a child, in that most difficult of situations, I was able to encounter a couple's deep faith, a faith so strong that they were able to share it with their other child, whose confirmation name will always remind her of the gift God gave to her and to her family and to me, if only for a brief time.

In my life as a priest, I have learned that sometimes grace comes not from my own efforts to help others find God's love in the difficult situations in life, but from the awesome way people's faith touches me and ends up ministering to me. Now, every time I hear the name *Gloria* or hear the "Gloria" sung, I am reminded of the faith of a family and their angel now in heaven, who is truly the glory of God. And because of that I am able to believe just a little bit more.

There have been many times in my priesthood when the tragedies whirling around me seemed almost too much to bear. Suicide, sudden death, the diagnosis of terminal illness—all these realities lead people to the priest, whom they look to for answers.

But there are no answers. My job is to remind those in grief that it is okay for them to feel what they are feeling. But I also challenge them not to forget or reject the truth that God loves them. How I am going to communicate this I don't know. I just take a deep breath and pray, asking God to pastor with me so that I can be helpful and healing.

33

The Gift of Trust

*The scandal that surrounds some priests has
affected the way all priests must now operate.*

EVERY TUESDAY MORNING we have Mass for
our parish school, so every Tuesday morning I
stand at the door of the church to greet the
children. And every Tuesday morning a little girl in the
second grade runs up the stairs and hugs my legs.

I remember a time when I would have lifted her up
into my arms and returned the innocent greeting. Now,
on the steps of a church that faces a busy street, I tap
her on the head, say "Good morning," and watch as she
goes inside.

Times have changed for priests, more than we might
realize. What people think about us has changed. And

thus how we respond must change as well. Some people still remain a grace to me, and for them I will be eternally grateful. The reasons why our relationships are what they are often rest on small incidents, comments, moments, and encounters rather than any big, dramatic events. The following story is about one family and a seemingly uneventful evening that was a great encouragement to me.

David and Megan came to St. Josaphat about the same time I did. They moved out after eight or so years to a bigger house in the suburbs. We still stay in contact, though their four children keep them quite busy. We share a special history. I witnessed and blessed the birth of their first son in their home. They allow me to be myself when I'm with them. When I was in the hospital, waiting for test results related to overwork and fatigue, they snuck in after visiting hours had ended and brought along the two things they knew would help me feel better: their baby daughter and a forbidden hot-fudge sundae with chocolate ice cream and whipped cream. I confess that both these things cheered me up. But of all our times together, one stands out above the rest.

They had invited me to their house for dinner. I especially enjoyed these dinners because they were breaks from rectory life and my not-too-healthy eating habits. Megan and David always prepared healthy meals, fresh and wholesome, that not only were enjoyable to eat but also made me feel good. This particular dinner was going to be really fresh, I gathered, because nothing had even been started on the stove or grill when I arrived.

I sat in the kitchen with Megan as she began to prepare the meal. With us were her two children, Joanie and little David, whose birth I had witnessed. We found ourselves talking about the current headlines about the church and priests. This was during the first round of scandals that shocked everyone in the early nineties. The immoral and wrong behavior of some priests had put all priests on the bubble. Neither priests nor the people of God knew what to make of what was unfolding. (We would continue to wonder what would play out in the media for close to a decade after this particular evening dinner.) As Megan and I waited for David to arrive home from work, she asked questions, and I tried as best I could to answer her.

Eventually, David called. He usually took public transportation home, but something had happened and Megan would have to pick him up. I offered to go in her place so that she could continue cooking and stay with the children. She flashed me a big smile. She had a better idea, she told me. The cooking could wait. Why didn't I just stay at the house and relax while she went to pick up David? I could spend the time with Joanie and little David, reading them stories. She asked her children if they would like that. They both clapped and jumped up and down in delight. She asked me if I would mind. Of course I wouldn't.

So she set us up in the living room, Joanie next to me on the sofa and David on my lap. We had a stack of books, some carrot sticks, and some juice to get us through the next half-hour or so. Megan left to pick up David. The kids and I read stories to each other and even made up a story to tell their mom and dad when they got home.

It was closer to an hour before they returned. They had stopped at the store to pick up fresh fruit for dessert and some fresh fish to grill. Megan figured that we'd be having a good time and wouldn't mind the delay.

We had a nice dinner, and the adults shared a bottle of wine. After dinner the children said their goodnights. I gave them a blessing. When David returned from taking them to their rooms, we sat and talked about the parish, about the church in general, and about the crisis in particular. I found myself listening a lot and answering the occasional question. I realized that most times when I talked about these issues with others, I felt tense and uncomfortable, but I was surprisingly at ease with Megan and David and much less defensive than I could have been.

Megan and David had trusted me that evening with the greatest gifts God had given them: their children. At a time when some people were choosing to look at priests with mistrust and doubt, they felt comfortable enough to leave their children with me. It was a meaningful way for them to communicate their trust in me. And they did so without having to utter a word.

As I left their house at the end of the night to walk back to the rectory, feeling full and loved and cared for and trusted, all I could do was turn to Megan and say softly, "Thanks for everything." She knew what for. She said nothing; she just kept smiling.

34

The Small Things

The best love happens in the small graces offered by others.

ONE YEAR, shortly after Easter, reporters from PBS followed me around for a week for a segment on *Religion and Ethics Newsweekly*. The format was "a day in the life of a priest." It was positive and supportive, designed to offset some of the sensational material everyone else was broadcasting. Still it caused a stir among some traditional Catholics who didn't like my responses. But by and large it received positive reactions and so I was glad I did it, even though I don't like watching myself on television. It is said that TV adds ten pounds. Well, I looked like a balloon that had escaped from the Macy's Thanksgiving Day Parade. It gave new meaning to the phrase "larger than life."

Because I knew that some people would respond negatively to the segment, I was somewhat concerned when I received a call from a man who said he had seen me on television and wanted to talk to me. He wouldn't give me his name, so I was worried it might be a crank. I was prepared for anything, but still I was shocked. The man on the line was a fifty-year-old Italian American from Cleveland who was leaving the next day to enter the seminary and start his studies for the priesthood. He had seen me on television and wanted to tell me before he began his quest that he hoped someday to be a priest like me, honest and open, but more important, unafraid to let his flaws and imperfections show. I think that was a compliment.

We had a nice conversation. He knew that the radical lifestyle change he was about to undertake would not be easy. And he had some doubts. I gave him the same advice a wise seminary professor had given me many years ago when he found me wandering the halls of the college seminary ready to pack my bags and go home. He told me that the seminary was not the priesthood. I stressed this to the new seminarian. Don't leave just because you don't like the seminary, I told him. Decide if you are called to be a priest, and if you are, just get through seminary. It is a means to an end. I invited him to use all that the seminary had to offer him in learning how to be pastoral with the people of God and inclusive and collaborative in ministry. I advised him not to get caught up in the politics infecting the church. I suggested that instead of arguing a position, he should spend his time learning how to be the best parish priest he could be.

Who knows where that seminarian's journey will take him? Who knows where the priesthood will lead women and men in the future? I am staying in it to find out.

It had been a mutually affirming conversation. He ended the call by observing that my priesthood appeared to fill me with joy. He was right. But sometimes I forget. Fatigued and overwhelmed, I forget. Self-pitying and attacked, I forget. It took a stranger on the phone to remind me.

Small things matter. Little graces, such as positive phone calls, can really help. I move now to another story of such a grace. By now you've probably figured out that I like to eat. This story, not surprisingly, involves food.

Most of us develop rewards that we fall back on after difficult situations or with which we pay ourselves back when no one else appreciates what we've done. If these rewards are healthy, they can be an added bonus. If they aren't, they need to be monitored. Their origins usually can be traced back to something in our childhood that remains with us and continues to make us feel good and comforted. I know that has been the case with me.

Since I was a child, hot-fudge sundaes have been more than comfort food for me. It all began in the second grade when I refused to come out of the boys' bathroom in school because I had flubbed a line in the Vocation Pageant. I remained in the bathroom until Mom came in and promised me that if I emerged we would go out for a hot-fudge sundae.

Hot-fudge sundaes do have a way of making everything all right. They are also good when I want to celebrate things that turned out better than I expected. Often they've symbolized success that came through no effort of my own but rather through God's actions or even through apparent failure—such as my misspoken line on stage those many years before.

My writing has gotten me invited to many parishes to give talks or to preach at their Lenten missions. At these events, I enjoy running into people with whom I have shared my ministry over the past three decades. I like seeing old familiar faces, renewing acquaintances, and, most of all, telling stories. In one of my mission talks, I shared the story of me, Mom, the pageant, the flubbed line, the bathroom, and the glorious conclusion that was the hot-fudge sundae.

At a parish near the Illinois-Wisconsin border where I was preaching a three-night Lenten mission, I ran into a number of people I knew from my days helping out at a parish in Waukegan, Illinois, when I was a seminarian. We were able to spend some time reminiscing about those long-gone days. On the last night, they invited me to go out with them after the talk for a little celebration. Despite facing an hour-and-a-half drive home, I eagerly accepted their invitation. We were to meet at a local restaurant that would still be open at that late hour.

When I arrived I found not only the people who had invited me but also at least a hundred other parishioners who had been in attendance at the missions. Every table in the restaurant was filled. And in front of every single person was a hot-fudge sundae. They had obviously gotten the message of my talk!

On that night I joyfully wolfed down the second-best hot-fudge sundae I'd ever had. Only the one my mom had bought me that fateful night forty-five years earlier could have tasted any better.

35

Echoes in an Empty Church

During very quiet moments after a church service, there remains a palpable energy, what I like to believe is a cloud of prayers— silent, spoken, sung, sobbed—that have yet to dissipate.

C HURCHES, LIKE PEOPLE, have their own histories, stories, and life spans. Sometimes, due to changing demographics, deteriorating buildings, dwindling contributions, or poor leadership, parishes are forced to close, their churches torn down or sold. It is a painful time for all involved. Remaining parishioners are reminded, usually by outsiders, that the church is, after all, not a building but the people of God. They are told that it is not right to place so much emphasis on the building. Instead they should simply focus on how much better everyone will feel worshiping in a more viable community.

I want to believe that. In fact, intellectually, I do. The problem is that deep in my gut I don't feel that way. I was in the position of being pastor of a parish that was reportedly on the verge of being forced to close. As I waited for the decision to be announced, I began to recognize the significance of such a decision and to consider how impossible it would be for me to carry it out. I prayerfully decided that if it came to that, I would resign my pastorate and leave the closure to someone else. I have since been told that such a position was the cowardly route. Maybe so. But I strongly felt that I was not appointed pastor to close a parish. That is not the work of a pastor. Give that job to the bureaucrats who make those decisions and who have never fallen in love with their people.

Fortunately, the parish and its beautiful church were spared, and I wasn't forced to carry out my decision, bad or good as it might have been. Due to the gentrification of the neighborhood that has taken place since then, the parish has grown significantly. This too produces a different and unique set of problems, one of which is the constantly increasing sacramental workload being placed on the shoulders of fewer ordained clergy.

It is not unusual on some weekends for me to spend most of my day in the church celebrating five Masses along with three weddings and a handful of baptisms. In addition, an RCIA or a CCD class may need to be taught or a marriage preparation program visited. If there is a family Mass that weekend, there will be hospitality after Mass—some time to share food, hot coffee, and conversation with the parishioners. This will get me through the next liturgy.

My life is like a race—I just look ahead to what is coming up next and focus all my energy on that. If I pause and take note of all that still needs to be done, I'll just quit, exhausted. I try to give everything my best. When I am finally able to grab the church key and lock up, a strange feeling comes over me. You would think that I would just want to leave quickly so that I could get back to my room, change my clothes, and either get on with my free afternoon or crash on the couch with a pint of ice cream. Instead, I'll lock the church doors and then sit in that quiet, sacred space that I have grown to love. I cherish those moments of sitting in that space alone. Everything around me looks a little beat-up. Wedding flowers are already starting to wilt. Bulletins that were probably read during my homily are strewn all over the pews and floors. Hymnals have not been returned to the racks. Cheerios crackle underfoot, a sign of the amazing number of toddlers fed in order to keep them quiet during Mass. The smells of candle wax and stale perfume linger in the air.

The church is profoundly quiet at those moments. Yet I feel what can only be described as a palpable energy in the air. I think of this energy as all the prayers—silent, spoken, sung, sobbed—that have been offered by so many people over the weekend and that have yet to dissipate. I sit there and let it all swirl around me until finally I am able to quiet myself, just as the church has quieted itself. At that moment, I seem to hear an almost inaudible sigh escaping in thanksgiving to the heavens. Did it come from me? Or was it released by this space, which has been made sacred by all who worshiped in it on this day?

My first experience of genuine sacred space was the chapel at Quigley High School Seminary. Modeled after Sainte Chapelle in Paris, with almost floor-to-ceiling stained-glass windows surrounded by solid Gothic brick, it became a safe haven in which I could get lost in thought and prayer. (The same feeling rushed over me when I later visited the actual Sainte Chapelle.) I remember being in the seminary chapel after spending the day with a group of classmates and a priest at the University of Chicago's folk music festival. We had taken an illegal swim in the school pool upon our return, and then we all gathered in the darkened chapel, where Fr. Al led us in prayer. There is space that not only is sacred but also envelops you in the sacred and makes you part of it. It happened for me then and still does today in different sacred places.

At those times in my church, I become aware of God's peace surrounding me and I realize that this is the right place for me to be—and to have been in all day. I am grateful that God has placed me here at this parish, grateful for all that we do here together, grateful for all that has happened among the people who have shared this sacred space with me. In spite of my long day and my need for rest, I need first to be in that empty church. In its echoes I find a deeper rest, and I can't leave just yet. I don't even want to.

Alone on Sunday Evening

I have tried to explain in this book why I am still a priest. I have no idea how these stories will be received. I feel that I've left more of myself on the pages of this book than on anything else I've written.

As I finish this writing, I feel much as I do on a typical Sunday evening, exhausted and all alone in my room at the rectory. Some men in this profession say that this is the most difficult time for them as priests—Sunday evening's solitude after a full day of intense involvement in peoples' lives. Once that workday is completed, an overwhelming sense of loneliness descends.

Sundays have a powerful emotional and spiritual impact on a priest. On that day, a priest will come into contact with 99 percent of the people to whom he will minister all week. A really pastoral priest will take advantage of the time he has with the congregation on the church steps before and after each Mass. Then there are the sermons themselves, which take a lot of energy and time to prepare, and also any and all meetings related to the congregation, from doughnut-filled hospitality time to religious-education classes and RCIA sessions. In addition there may be an evening Mass to celebrate or an emergency hospital visit to make. Some parishes even schedule social functions on Sundays. But usually, by late Sunday evening, a very long day is finally over.

My nephew lived in the rectory with me one summer while he was in medical school nearby. It was a good way for us to be around each other a bit more. At the end of the summer he wrote me a thank-you, saying how nice it had been to get to know me better. Until that summer I had just been his priest uncle who ate pasta with the family on Sunday afternoons (when we were able to gather) and then fell asleep. That was an accurate description of what my family had seen of me over the years.

One Sunday afternoon a few years ago, I noticed a deacon who interned at our parish looking so down and overwhelmed that I was compelled to ask what was wrong. He had finished a successful day: he had given an on-the-mark homily at two Masses, had taught a great RCIA class, and had celebrated a touching baptism. Parishioners, especially the young adults, had hovered around him, inviting him to their new houses for dinners that would be served on never-before-used wedding-gift china.

But while he was sitting alone in his room he started thinking about his former girlfriend and suddenly experienced a loneliness that he'd never felt before. So I welcomed him—a young man not yet ordained to the priesthood—to the Sunday evening world of the celibate priest. We needed to talk strategy—for overcoming, or at least getting through, these emotional times. We talked about taking long naps, visiting family, reading, going to movies, gathering with other priests, even writing (as I am now doing). While the strategies themselves were kind of lame, we were able to talk about the source of the struggle. I tried to assure him that Sunday evenings were the toughest times for even the best priests.

Sunday night loneliness, I told him, comes with Sunday morning affirmation and intimacy. The people of God affirm us in so many ways on Sundays. They are there. They listen. They respond. They volunteer. They give. They ask. And they also touch us physically, embracing and kissing us. We priests receive more attention on a Sunday morning than most of the rest of the world gets in an entire workweek. And it can become as addictive as anything else. My priestly life is wrapped up in the lives of many others in intimate ways. This is a large portion of the reward for the lifestyle I have embraced.

But Sunday is over quickly, and all those other lives move on. They have other things to do, so our Sundays with them melt away. Then we priests are often left to face Sunday evenings alone. For some, these become times of acute temptation. And for those few who cannot overcome their weaknesses, what began as a somewhat positive "addiction" to interaction with others becomes replaced by other addictions—including those to sex or substances. These addictions won't end the loneliness, and in fact the added guilt they bring will make that loneliness all the more unbearable. A vicious cycle begins.

Some priests handle this loneliness in sublime and positive ways, but most of the priests I know stumble through Sunday evenings as best they can—exhausted and thus grateful for sleep when it comes. While we wait for sleep, our minds fill up with questions about our ministry: *What more could I have done in that situation? Why didn't I do this or that differently? How could I have forgotten that? Why did that person respond like that?* In this way, we wrestle with demons of our own creation.

Or maybe we wrestle with the same angel that visited Jacob. Jacob and the angel struggled all night before Jacob left limping—and renamed. Jacob the man with many shortcomings became Israel the patriarch after Abraham and Isaac, the father of God's people.

Maybe I, the very human priest, need the lonely Sunday evening so that I will wake up on Monday morning the "wounded healer" that Henri Nouwen says I must become. As I am wounded I become worthy to be called "priest of God."

So on this Sunday night I leave you these final reflections. Know this: God is *still* calling me by name. I find both intimacy and loneliness in that call. I'll survive the loneliness, just as I have survived the deaths of my parents, my mentor, my spiritual director, and my closest priest friends over the years of my ministry. The intimacy afforded me by my ministry not just on Sundays but every day is, and will continue to be, what keeps me going.

What will the God who calls me by name ask me to do—and be—tomorrow? I don't know. But I will wake up Monday morning, and Sunday evening will be over for at least a week. And God will call me to serve and to love in whatever way God chooses.

Here I *still* am, Lord. Dominic is here to do your will.

A Thank-You to Good People

I love my life as a priest. I love it as any person must learn to love his or her life, accepting the difficulties and sad times, savoring and remembering the blessings and good times.

A huge part of that love is simple gratitude. Yes, I'm grateful to God for my life and for the grace God provides for living it. But I am also grateful to many people. Some of them turn up in stories, but many of them don't—or haven't yet. At the end of this book of stories and reflections, I include some descriptions of the people in whom God lives and through whom God does such wonderful work.

The Women

In an off-the-highway antique store somewhere in central Illinois, I found an old framed print dated 1919. Its heading reads "Women of the Bible." It contains eight oval, sepia-toned portraits all in a row, including Ruth and Rebecca and ending with Mary of Magdala and

Mary the mother of Jesus. It must have hung in a religious Protestant home or in a small Bible church, given that Mary the mother of Jesus appears simply as the last among equals, with nothing to distinguish her in any way. We Catholics would have shown our special respect for Mary by setting her apart from and above the rest. The print now hangs in the sacristy of our church for all to see, especially our many women volunteers.

My life as a priest has been enriched by women whose faith rivals that of these good women from the pages of sacred Scripture. Unfortunately most people, including Catholics, are not as familiar with these biblical women as we should be. One reason might be that they seem to be excluded from the Sunday and weekday cycles of Mass readings, which for too many of us are the extent of our exposure to the Bible. It can be argued that woman and their role throughout the history of God's people have never been fully celebrated and still are not. Recently I saw Bill Moyers interview the head of the National Conference of Catholic Bishops on PBS. I smiled ruefully as I watched him skirt the issue of women's ordination by stating the church's commitment to have women in leadership roles. I knew he could never publicly advocate the ordination of women.

What surprises and challenges me is that, given this climate, women rich in faith are still able to live out their beliefs so powerfully and effectively. And even more surprising, they have enough faith in reserve to be there for me and for so many other men when we need them.

Italians and other nationalities believe that a priest's mother automatically earns heaven. Well, I know from the depths of my heart that my mother certainly did not need any help from me in getting St. Peter to swing open the pearly gates for her. Her life was a constant education for me on how to be generous, caring, compassionate, and loving and how not to hurt another person even if he or she has hurt me. I am a very slow learner. Mom died just a few months ago, and I find that I continue to learn from my memories of her.

Ruby, my "other mother," also died recently. She was my confidante, my spiritual director, and my accountant. Consequently, she knew me better than anyone else did. She spent twenty-seven years being an example to me of letting go and trusting in God. I often fought her and resisted her advice. Her last words to me, uttered as she held my hands tightly the day before she died, were an attempt to get me to trust as she did. I've tried, but it has not been easy, especially now that she is gone.

Then there is Maureen, unafraid to challenge injustice wherever she finds it, be it in the church and its hierarchy or in self-righteous parishioners, or even in fatal diseases. She defies categorization. She never gives up. And when I start viewing my situation through comfortable clerical eyes, she forces me to see things from a totally different perspective. But then she is there to help me once I realize how impotent or self-serving I have become.

Teresa, the hardworking mother of a large family, always finds the time despite her physical ailments and concerns to be of service at her parish, working with pastors and others patiently. She makes herself available to a larger community of unwed mothers and their families, to a number of priests, to neighbors and friends. Her goodness comes so naturally that after a while it can be taken for granted. Yet her strong faith shines brightly through all that she does.

There are the women who serve the church in essential ways. Parishes, schools, and other organizations would not survive without them. Pat works very hard at supporting all the priests she believes in and trusts and loves, although some of us can be very high-maintenance. Mary has been much more than the secretary for the Association of Chicago Priests. She has been invaluable to those of us who have chaired that august group. She genuinely cares about people and puts her concerns into action. Betty is principal of the parish school and someone I truly respect. It is a blessing to work with her. Her consistently Christian responses encourage me to live with more integrity and compassion.

All of these are women of prayer and of deep faith. They are intelligent. They have endured difficult life experiences and have become better people for them. They instinctively gather others around them and form communities. Their creative energy constantly regenerates the ministry that surrounds them. I often wonder how they are able to keep going forward and never give up.

These women surely mirror those courageous women found in Scripture with their own style of courage. I know that I cannot let them down. (In any case, I would not want to face their righteous anger.) I know they will always set me straight, each in her own way. I need these good women, whose witness is bringing about the changes, slowly but surely, that the Holy Spirit mandates to happen through their lives. This is a force that nothing can stop.

The Good Old Guys

More than anything or anyone else in my life, they give me hope. I watch them and I am amazed by their openness and their capacity to work even at their advanced age. My guess is that their openness and flexibility are products of their having lived through and experienced so many changes in their priesthood. At the same time, that old-fashioned work ethic they had when they were ordained has remained with them, and so the privilege of ministry still motivates them.

When I begin to fret over the future in general or about my own future in particular, I look to these men. I see them functioning with such quiet grace that I become confident that there is still growth awaiting me, if only I can remain open to it.

As I write this, Matty is not well. He is in a nursing home. There is a good chance that he won't live to read these words. He is truly a priest's priest. One bishop frequently tells about the high school seminary canoe trips he went on years ago with Matty and others that cemented his vocation. Matty always brought out the best in people by being so positive. He always had a supportive word for a priest who needed it—and he always meant it. A portrait of him hangs in the rectory of St. Teresa Parish, where he was pastor. In it he is smiling, surrounded by parishioners of seemingly every age and nationality. He worked hard not only in this parish but also in a number of parishes, even when he was well past retirement age. At gatherings of fellow priests he always had his camera so he could capture the moment. My favorite story about him is of the time he went skiing in his advanced years and realized he had taken a lift to a hill that was too difficult for him. So he wrapped himself around his skis and poles and rolled down the hill. Here was a man who clearly knew how to adjust to his circumstances.

John is a common name, so the St. Johns of the world usually have a descriptive title to help distinguish them from one another, such as "the Evangelist" or "the Baptist" or "of the Cross." This John would have to be known as "the Listener." He has been a spiritual director for many, pastor of two fortunate congregations, and mentor of many priests and seminarians. John listens so well that his responses are ultimately very challenging. He is just now entering retirement. But his priesthood will continue, because he won't stop listening. As a talker, I get worried when I spend time with him, thinking that I've said too much. It would do me good to learn to listen as John does.

Bill worked in a diocesan Office of Catholic Education. He was also a seminary rector. But I will always hold him up as the standard of what it means to be a pastor. I watched him make it look so simple as I assisted him at St. Germaine Parish on weekends while I taught in the seminary. He empowered people and showed his trust in them by the decisions he made. Quite often when I have found myself in a difficult situation as a pastor or have had a tough decision to make, I've thought, *What would Bill do in this situation?* His example has guided me on so many occasions. He is retired now, but he is still skilled at reading people's hearts with insight and honesty. I recently experienced this when Bill heard me preach a homily I was struggling with. He sent me an e-mail afterward, having figured out what was really bothering me, what I hadn't been able to say. What a skill for a priest to have.

I've written about Gene previously. He is the number-one reason I am a priest today. He is the reason I went to the seminary. When I run into him now I am amazed by his still-youthful enthusiasm and appearance. Age has not dulled his priesthood at all. I realize that his sense of humor, which is always self-deprecating and never directed toward others, is certainly one of the factors that keep him so young. And that really gives me hope.

At his wake and funeral, a picture of Jack was handed out, showing him surrounded by children releasing multicolored balloons into the air. Throughout his life, Jack was labeled the "radical." But he was much more than that. Jack's strength was his constant openness to new ideas and to the Spirit interacting with him in new ways. Because he was naturally filled with hope, he fought against forces that threatened to block people's ability to use their God-given talents. Such an attitude often got Jack in trouble with authorities, both civil and religious. But he knew he had to make those balloons soar.

I've mentioned only a few priests out of a large fellowship of men dedicated to their callings. These men represent the best of the priesthood and what is immutable about it. They are the heroes who were sharing their ministry before it was popular to do so. Now, as a new generation of priests tries to lead us back to a clericalism that should be dead, these older priests proclaim with their lives that their priesthood is not passé or a failed experiment. Far from it. They are role models that should be lifted up and never forgotten.

I can't help but wonder how much richer the priesthood would be if the richness of another gender had been part of its history and evolution. What we have lost! Yet the women in our faith continue to respond to the call that God gives us all—to respond to the needs of people with strength and compassion. And through their service they challenge everyone to explore what God's call means in every life and to allow God's love to come forth. Each of us must learn what it means to be baptized. We all share in the priesthood of Jesus Christ.

The Very Good Sisters

This morning after Mass, one of the Daughters of Charity who worships regularly at the parish came and told me that she had been transferred to New York, where she would be working with the poor as part of a team of five nuns. While I will miss seeing her in the pews, I have one image to carry with me always. It was the rededication of our church. At the end of that beautiful liturgy, hoarse with a terrible cold, I congratulated the people. When I said, "You did it!" the church rang out with applause. As people stood and cheered, this sister simply turned and hugged the person next to her. It was a wonderful moment for the church.

My life and my ministry have been enhanced by the lives of many women religious. They have supported and taught me. Most of them journeyed through the sweeping changes of Vatican II, and they came out more whole than the rest of us, perhaps because they had taken its message to heart early on.

Sr. Innocentia, R.S.M., visited my mother back when nuns were not supposed to even leave the convent, helping her through an agonizing depression following the death of my sister. Because of Sr. Innocentia helping my mother through a most difficult pregnancy, I was born. I literally owe my life to this nun, and so my priesthood as well. I am told that when the neighborhood and parish grew poorer, she not only welcomed those disadvantaged families into its school but also found them food and clothing. Many, including me, consider her a saint.

Sr. Mary Therese Harrington, S.H., taught me that our faith is shared, and she did so through human experience and not with memorized doctrine. She put a human face on the spiritual through her adaptation of techniques used for teaching the faith to children with disabilities. And she laughed as she did it, trusting us naive seminarians to learn from her. She continues this work four decades later. I have become the storyteller I am partly because of her.

My first parish assignment could easily be described as a train wreck. I served with a pastor whose view of life was so dramatically different from mine that it was impossible for us to share the ministry. Consequently, I found that I spent as much time in the parish convent with the nine School Sisters of Notre Dame as I did in the rectory. When the pastor would not let the sisters take the car that the parish had bought them on an overnight trip to the motherhouse for a meeting (he often treated them like children), I gave them mine to use. And I dared him to try and tell me what to do with my property. In turn, the sisters were there for me, leaving me thermoses of hot toddies and finding someone to replace me for morning Mass the day after my grandmother's funeral (it was the pastor's day off). Two of them just celebrated fifty years of ministry, Sr. Donata and Sr. Dorothy, and they still make me laugh.

Sr. Helen Marshall, O.P., taught me how I could be both professional and caring in my ministry and how those qualities complemented each other. She was the academic dean when I was teaching. I always took Helen's critical remarks to heart. Her insights and her honesty taught me how to teach. With her determination to work even as her eyesight failed, she also taught me how not to give up and how to use what God gives us to the fullest. Her death has left a void in my heart. I cherish the memories of the house Masses held with the other sisters in her simple apartment. She constantly empowered me and taught me that empowering others is an essential part of ministry.

Sr. Patricia Crowley, O.S.B., had a vision and dedicated her life to making it a reality. Deborah's Place is one of the finest programs for homeless women in the country, and Sr. Patricia has gathered the best women in the city to work with her. She challenges me never to forget the needs of those who are invisible in our society. It was a privilege to work with her and to support her when she battled city hall and came away with a great victory.

The Daughters of Charity, the Little Sisters of the Poor, the Sisters of the Holy Family of Nazareth, and the Sisters of Mercy are all communities who continue to support my priesthood. When I see their selfless dedication, I am greatly inspired to strive always to be better at what I am called to do.

I save one sister for last: Sister Phillipa Coogan, B.V.M. She taught me how to write by constantly pushing me to say what I wanted to say, clearly and simply. I know that I still fail at it frequently. I shudder to remember how she critiqued some of my sentences in front of class. But when I visited her years later, she told me to use my writing as part of my priesthood. She assured me that if I was honest with it, I could make a difference. Then she told me to be bold in what I wrote, but to be careful in the words I used. She ended her advice with her patented wink. I hope that what I write will always live up to her high standards.

So many sisters have raised the bar by their example. They are much more than the "good sisters"—as we called them—of the past. They were and are among these "very good sisters" who are leading the church into the future.